MW00603874

Cool

Road Trips

in SW Florida

Kim Cool

Kim Cool

HISTORIC VENICE PRESS

Cool

Road Trips

in SW Florida

Kim Cool

HISTORIC VENICE PRESS

Also by Kim Cool:
Ghost Stories of Venice
Ghost Stories of Sarasota
Circus Days in Sarasota & Venice
Ghost Stories of Clearwater & St. Petersburg

Cool Road Trips in SW Florida

© 2005 Kim Cool
Cover photo by Marianna Csizmadia
Map segments @2005 Navteq, used with permission of the
publisher.

All rights reserved. No part of this book may be reproduced or
transmitted in any form or by any means, electronic or
mechanical, including photocopying, recording or by any
informational storage or retrieval system, except by a reviewer
who may quote brief passages in a review to be printed in a
magazine or newspaper, without permission in writing from
the publisher.

For information, contact:
Historic Venice Press
P. O. Box 800
Venice, FL 34284
941.468-6556
kimcool@www.historicvenicepress.com

First Edition 2005
Printed in the United States of America
ISBN   0-9721655-6-8

Dedication

This one is for my Web master and favorite daughter, Heidi Adams Coventry Cool, for my special friend Charles J. Adams III, who started me on this circuitous road and for Dennis Gardner who not only pushed me to do this first road trip book but also offered invaluable suggestions toward the cover art and the book's content.

Thank you all for being there for me.

Contents

Part 3 Check out the Culture Coast... 73

Part 4 Discover the Platinum Coast... 109

Cool trippin' over Venice with Curt Warren, 2004 US Hang Gliding Champion

Photo courtesy of Warren Windsports www.warrenwindsports.com

Introduction

One road trip leads to another.

For whatever reason, my life has been a succession of road trips, and even a few railroad trips. My parents took me on the first ones to beaches and amusement parks in and around the Cleveland, Ohio area where I was raised. Many a weekend we would travel somewhere from our home in Shaker Heights. One day we might take a short ride to visit the Cleveland Museum of Art. On another day we might visit Geauga Lake Amusement Park in Aurora. On yet another day we might head out to see the county fair in Geauga County or visited Amish country in Middlefield. We took the train to Chicago and New York.

Sometimes we took a few photos, but mostly we collected the memories in our heads.

If we traveled farther afield, to a different state, we still made road trips, to explore whatever place we visited.

A pattern was developing.

By the time I arrived at Sweet Briar College in Amherst County, Virginia, I was hooked. Even as a carless freshman I managed road trips to Charlottesville, Lexington, Hot Springs for skiing, Lynchburg for shopping and even short jaunts to nearby Amherst, which, in those days, had little more than a general store. We went most places by train from the Sweet Briar Station, traveling on the Southern Railroad.

As a college sophomore I wrote my first travel articles. Little did I know that years later I would change careers to become a full-time journalist and part-time collector of ghost stories as one road, indeed, led to another.

In 1993, I made the longest road trip of my life, moving from Ohio to Venice, Florida, otherwise known as the Sharks Tooth Capital of the World. That the Brotherhood of Locomotive Engineers had a hand in its history as well is of note to railroad buffs.

Venice is a great location from which to take road trips. My first ones were to the local beaches — the sharks teeth strewn beaches of Venice and the white sugar sand beach on nearby Siesta Key in Sarasota.

As a newcomer to the state, a trip to Marie Selby Botanical Gardens was necessary to learn about tropical gardening.

Then there were trips north to the Dali Museum in St. Petersburg, south to the Botanical Gardens in Naples and east to Orlando and its many attractions.

When I was not counting sand at the beach or driving the highways and byways of Florida, I was settling into my new career with the Venice Gondolier Sun, working my way through the editorial department from one position to another while getting to know my adopted city and state. By the time I became travel and leisure editor, I knew I had found my niche. I could spend my days writing about everything I liked to do, from attending plays and the opera to visiting theme parks, hang gliding over Venice and having tea at places as diverse as the Ritz-Carlton in Naples to a tiny British tea shop in Sarasota. I was able to go behind the scenes at Busch Gardens, Sea World and Walt Disney World. I was able to attend the wedding of Shrek at Universal and eat breakfast with Goofy and Chip & Dale and other characters at Walt Disney World. When WDW opened its Mission Space ride, I was one of the first passengers, seated next to the director of NASA and one of the ride's designers. When the MGM Studios redid its Tower of Terror, I was there, randomizing the tower experience, I was there.

When the Portofino Bay Hotel opened at Universal Orlando, I was there, almost too short to climb into its big comfy beds. I flew in a balloon over Cypress Gardens before it closed and was one of the first to cheer when that classic road trip destination reopened late in 2004, after surviving near bankruptcy and four hurricanes.

Week after week I wrote about my adventures in the Venice Gondolier Sun, which eventually published a booklet entitled "Day Trippin' With Kim Cool," earning two awards from the Florida Press Association. About that time that I went into road trip overdrive, hunting ghost stories while continuing to explore my new state, wearing out my ancient Dodge and acquiring a new Tracker.

In the course of my job, I was able to return to the rails. I traveled on the Venice-Simplon Orient Express from Verona, Italy, to London and across Canada on the American Orient Express. Those trips rekindled my love affair with railroad trips. I found more railroad destinations in SW Florida. Whether guided by guardian angels, new friends or old ghosts, the time had come to assemble Cool Road Trips in SW Florida. I hope you enjoy the result of my road work.

Kim Cool

Venice, Florida
June 2005

Part I
Trippin' along I-4

Photo courtesy of Universal Orlando

Photo courtesy of Bok Tower Gardens

The top third of Bok Tower houses the 57-bell carillon. From Interstate 75, take Exit 257 (SR 60) at Brandon. Proceed east to lake Wales and follow the signs to Bok Tower Gardens. Go north on SR 17 (do not confuse this with US 17, which also runs north and south but is some 16 miles west of Lake Wales) and east on Burns Ave. to the gardens. For more information, including hours and prices, call (863) 676-1408.

Bok Tower Gardens

Bok Tower and its famous 57-bell singing carillon tower was designed by Lyman Phillips of the Frederick Law Olmsted firm, which designed Central Park, the campus of Stanford University and many of the most famous gardens in America during the late 19th century. This Florida creation stands apart from other attractions in the state. The gardens were designed by Frederick Law Olmsted Jr.

Carillon concerts by a live carilloneur are presented each afternoon. At other times, recorded carillon music can be heard throughout the gardens.

Holland-born Edward Bok bestowed the gardens on his adopted country in honor of the success he had here. The 205-foot tall tower housing the carillon bells sits atop the highest point in Florida, 298 feet above sea level.

Each afternoon there is a live concert by the resident carilloneur, one of very few in the entire United States. At other times and at half hour intervals, recorded carillon music is played. It can be heard throughout the gardens. Simplicity and serenity are words that come to mind in relation to the gardens and the 12,900-square-foot Mediterranean Revival home, added to the tower property in 1970. In contrast, the neo-Gothic tower with art deco influences is a study in intricate workmanship and in the variety of textures and details incorporated in its design.

The house was recently opened to tourists and is especially stunning when decorated by professional designers for the winter holidays. Gardens surrounding the home were designed with flowers in shades of blue, white and yellow, colors used in the Tunesian tiles adorning the house.

Bok Tower Gardens is owned and maintained by the American Foundation, a nonprofit corporation created by Bok in 1923 to direct his philanthropic enterprises.

Photo by Kim Cool

Topiaries are larger at Cypress Gardens Adventure Park at Lake Wales.

From Orlando, take I-4 west to Exit 55 (Highway 27 South), At SR 540, head west 4 miles. From Tampa, take I-4 east to Polk Parkway East. Turn left on Highway 17, then right at SR 540 (Cypress Gardens Boulevard). The gardens will be 3 miles ahead on the right. For more information, call (863) 324-2111 or visit www.cypressgardens.com.

Cypress Gardens

Ravaged by time and competition, Cypress Gardens closed in 2003. The 2004 hurricanes pummeled Florida adding to the gardens' woes on the eve of its reopening. But nothing could destroy this attraction. In late fall 2004, Florida's famed Cypress Gardens was reborn and reopened.

The water ski capital of the world, the new Cypress Gardens, features a comedy show, "Pirates of Cypress Cove," ice skating shows in the Royal Palm Theater, nightly 3-D and laser light shows over Lake Eloise, a host of new rides such as those found at its sister park in Valdosta, Ga., Wild Adventures Theme Park, and a new Splash Island Water Park, similar to a water park of the same name at Wild Adventures.

The majestic Banyan tree, which grew from a 1939 seedling, is living proof of the park's will to survive against an influx of competing attractions unheard of when the gardens, Southern belles in hoop skirts and pyramid water skiers made their debut at the first theme park in Florida.

Esther Williams was filmed there in a pool especially built for her. Elvis Presley performed there. So did Johnny Carson. Visitors bought miles of film to capture images of the gardens and the girls. The photos were shown in living rooms in Indiana, Ohio, New York and many other places around the world. Today's visitors have all that and more as the new owner continues to add topiary animals, a butterfly garden called the Wings of Wonder, rides and new shows.

Thirty-seven exciting rides, including four roller coasters and the world's tallest spinning rapids ride, offer today's visitors something their grandparents never had at the original Cypress Gardens.

More than 40 all-star concerts are scheduled each year. Seasonal events also are in the planning stages.

Photo courtesy of Dolly Parton Dixie Stampede

A Roman rider astride two horses jumps through a flaming hoop during the Dolly Parton Dixie Stampede Dinner Show.

Take Interstate 4 to Exit 68 toward Lake Buena Vista and merge onto Vineland Avenue. The Dolly Parton Dixie Stampede will be at 8251 Vineland. For more information, or to make reservations for the dinner show, call (407) 238-2777.

Dolly Parton's Dixie Stampede

You get more than you bargain for at Dolly Parton's Dixie Stampede in Orlando. Even before the dinner show begins, there is an opening act in the Carriage Room.

You sit at long tables in the Carriage Room, with barely enough room for a person to walk between the tables and benches and then, all of a sudden, Australia's Electric Cowboy Greg Anderson, comes down the steps from the small stage in that room — on his horse, a quarter horse stallion named Starstruck.

Both horse and rider are lit up with electric lights. As this warm up act continues, the pair ride up and down the narrow aisles while Anderson belts out a collection of country tunes. Did I mention that Starstruck climbs stairs, and that this is only the opening act, something to watch while nibbling on popcorn and peanuts and sipping a soft drink, beer or wine.

From the Carriage Room, the audience progresses into the 35,000-square foot arena for the dinner show. Tables are set in tiers around the perimeter of the arena and what must be the fastest wait staff anywhere serves up dinner faster than the show's horse can gallop.

Dinner includes a whole rotisserie chicken, barbecued pork loin, vegetable soup, biscuit, corn on the cob, potato, dessert and beverage. There is a vegetarian selection, if desired. Both meals come with dessert.

The main show features Palomino and quarter horse breeds plus Appaloosas and Paints, trained to turn on a dime, jump through flaming hoops, ride in formation and support the amazing stunt riders as they do things no one can do on horse-back.They do it anyway.

Take home a souvenir boot mug to remember the adventure known as the Dixie Stampede.

Photo by KIm Cool

Fantasy of Flight is the place to see one-of-a-kind rare WWII aircraft such as a P-51 Mustang, a Grumman Wildcat and a B-24 Liberator.

From Interstate 4, take Exit 44 (Polk City) and head north to the stop light. Turn left and watch for the red and white checked water tower. The entrance is at 1400 Broadway Blvd. S.E. Parking is free and plentiful. For more information, call (863) 984-3500 or visit www.fantasyofflight.com.

Fantasy of Flight

If you see an airplane with its nose in the ground and its tail in the air, you will know you are near Fantasy of Flight.

Should you want to emulate that flight or, preferably one with a happier ending, you may do so at one of Florida's more unusual tourist attractions.

In addition to getting up close to vintage aircraft, at Fantasy of Flight near Polk City, visitors can take the controls of several different types of planes. The controls are in combat simulators. You can fly as many missions as you dare. Or, you can take the controls of an ultralight, with the help of a pilot, to soar above Fantasy of Flight. In the Great Balloon Experience, passengers are lifted 600 feet into the air on a tethered balloon, which offers a view stretching some 25 miles on a clear day. The best part is your descent will not be to a watermelon patch two hours away, but right back to your take-off spot, saving you time for more flight adventures.

Begin with the self-guided tour. You will be transported back to the era of World War II from an aviation viewpoint.

Among the planes on display is the actual Ford Tri-Motor used in the film, "Indiana Jones and the Temple of Doom." The collection is said to be the world's largest private collection and includes more than 20 signature aircraft. There is a B-24 Liberator and a British Spitfire plus a B-17 Flying Fortress.

Should you work up an appetite while flying one or more missions in Fightertown, a visit to the Compass Rose Restaurant is in order. Modeled after a 1930s era diner, the Compass Rose offers breakfast and lunch items true to the period.

The gift shop is packed with what may well be the largest selection of aviation-themed merchandise of any such shop in the United States. You can even buy an engine.

Fantasy of Flight is open daily. Hours may vary by season.

Photo by Kim Cool

The Annie Pfeiffer Chapel was designed by Frank Lloyd Wright for Florida Southern College. Interior of bell tower above.

From Interstate 4, travel east to Exit 18, then south to Florida Avenue in Lakeland. Continue south to McDonald Street. Turn left and continue to the intersection with Johnson Avenue. The library will be the nearest building. Park in any of its parking lots. Begin and end your tour at the library. For more information, call (941) 680-4111 or visit www.flsouthern.edu.

Florida Southern College

The Wright stuff is in Lakeland.

On the campus of Florida Southern College is the largest collection of the work by architect Frank Lloyd Wright to be found on one site.

It was no April Fool's joke when FSC president Dr. Ludd Spivey telegrammed the architect on April 1, 1938. Having read Wright's biography, Spivey appealed to the man's ego, offering him the opportunity to create a "great education temple in Florida."

Six weeks later, with student effort, little money and World War II emerging, ground was broken for what would become a 20-year project to complete just 8 of the 18 planned buildings. The campus is the only example anywhere of Wright's community planning concept, which was to decentralize the city by distributing urban functions to rural areas and to utilize new building ideas.

The first was the Annie Pfeiffer Chapel, dedicated three years later. That one building contains all the basic elements of Wright design. Three seminar buildings were finished in the next two years. Separated by courtyards, the seminar buildings featured skylights and inlaid glass walls. The library was dedicated in 1945 as Spivey's dream gradually became reality.

Today, named in honor of college benefactor William M. Hollis, the room houses the Frank Lloyd Wright Visitor Center and Esplanade Gift Shop. Wright's geometric influence can be seen throughout the building.

Last to be built was the Polk County Science Building, containing the only Wright-designed planetarium ever built.

The college was recognized by U.S. News & World Report as one of the Five Top Regional Liberal Arts Colleges in the South.

Photo by Kim Cool

Gatorland performers prepare for their next show.

Take Interstate 75 to Exit 261 (I-4) Travel east to the Oseola Parkway. Follow the parkway to Highway 441 and travel north to Gatorland, which is 7 miles south of the Florida Mall between the 417 Greenway and the Oseola Parkway, For more information, including hours and prices, call (407) 855-5496 or (800) 393-JAWS (5297).

Gatorland

When roadside attractions were as prevalent as Burma-Shave signs, Owen Godwin opened Gatorland. It was 1949.

The Burma-Shave signs are gone, but Gatorland remains. The attraction survived the arrival of the giant theme parks and remains one of the most intriguing Florida attractions.

Gatorland is a hands-on, eco-tourist destination where visitors can see hundreds of alligators and crocodiles in their native environments. Visitors also can witness a few "hand-to-claw" contests that pit gators versus gator grapplers.

More than a roadside attraction, today's Gatorland, with help from the University of Florida, is a research center and alligator farm. Once endangered, the gators are thriving in a disease-free environment and special breeding marsh.

Also to be found at Gatorland are thousands of migratory birds, perched high in the trees. Walkways above the water bring the visitors up close to the nesting birds and keep birds and people safe from the gators swimming below.

Take a morning walk on the boardwalk. Stop for lunch at Pearl's Kitchen, located at the end of the boardwalk. Try the gator tail nuggets, gator ribs, hamburgers, hot dogs or chicken.

After lunch, catch a show such as gator wrestlin' or the gator jumparoo where giant gators leap from the water for a chicken held 2 or 3 feet above the water. Some of these alligators have performed since the day Gatorland opened to the public. There also are snake and crocodile shows and exhibits, including a nursery with perfect conditions for baby crocodiles.

Visitors can work with Gatorland animal handlers to experience the swamp and field up close. Gatorland offers Cypress Glades Airboats and Adventure Tours for those who want to view Central Florida's swamp life in its natural state.

Closing times and show schedules vary by season.

Photo by Kim Cool

Leu Gardens has something in bloom in every season.
From Interstate 4, take Exit 43 (Princeton Road) east to
U.S. 17-92 (Mills Avenue). Go south on U.S. 17-92, turning left on
Virginia Drive. Follow Virginia east to Forest. Leu Gardens will
be on your left at 1920 N. Forest Ave. There is good signage all
the way from I-4. For more information, call (407) 246-2620 or
visit. www.leugardens.org.

Leu Gardens

Camellias fill Leu Gardens with color each January. The multi-hued display lasts through March.

Then come the roses, vegetables and herbs — something for every season. Since gifted to the city of Orlando by Harry P. and Mary Leu in 1961, the camellia plants have grown to tree size. Other specialty gardens were added and matured on the 40-acre site. Developed by the Leus over 25 years, the gardens are a repository for thousands of specimen plants from all over the world, everything from camellias to cacti. The former Leu home is listed on the National Register of Historic Places and was restored in the 1980s. It is open for hourly tours.

Well traveled, the Leus always came home with plants and seeds, especially camellias, Harry Leu's favorite plant. Because of the near perfect growing conditions in Leu's Orlando garden, the collection became one of the finest in the United States. Live oaks protect the plants from the brutal summer heat.

Displays change with the seasons. A recent addition is the home demonstration garden complex, which includes 10 distinct gardens designed to showcase garden design, techniques and environmental interests of Central Florida.

The formal rose garden is centered by a fountain. An adjacent patio area often is the site of garden weddings.

Palms, cycads, bamboo, daylilies, annuals and wetland plants each has a special area within the garden complex along Lake Rowena. Butterfly, herb and vegetable gardens provide inspiration. The tropical stream garden provides another type of serene garden setting.

Leu Gardens is open daily from 9 a.m.-5 p.m. and until 8 p.m. during the months when daylight savings time is in effect. On Sundays during that time period, the gardens close at 6 p.m.

Photo courtesy of Medieval Times

Trained steeds and their riders star in a colorful Medieval pageant as guests enjoy a banquet in the castle.

From Interstate 4, take Exit 64 A (Highway 192 East). Travel east 6 miles. Medieval Times is between Guide markers 14 and 15. For more information, visit www.medievaltimes.com or call (407) 396-2900 or (800) 229-8300.

Medieval Times

Nothing like jousting for the best table at dinner.

At Orlando's Medieval Times, other folks do the jousting and you do the eating.

Picture yourself in an 85,000-square-foot European-Style castle. It is 900 years ago. Chivalry was more than a word and jousting tournaments were a regular event. Kings and queens needed entertainment, colorful and sometimes bloody entertainment featuring all the knights of the realm in full regalia, on their gallant steeds. There would be jousting and sword fights and battles to the death.

At Medieval Times, the pageantry remains. Only the blood and gore are gone. Before 1,100 dinner guests seated around the show ring, 100 costumed Medieval characters will perform with beautiful Andalusian horses.

The riders and horses replicate tournament games of old, display their agility while jousting and eventually participating in an exciting battle, ending with just one winner.

As the show progresses, so does the banquet feast.

Served by serfs and wenches in period costumes, the meal consists of an appetizer, fresh vegetable soup, roasted chicken, spare rib, potatoes, pastry and libations. There is a vegetarian alternative, available on request The meal is eaten as it would have been 900 years ago, without silverware.

Dinner and the show last about two hours. The doors open 90 minutes before showtime, which varies according to the season.

Complementing the castle is a working village, called Medieval Life, which employs skilled artisans who work as carpenters,s blacksmiths, potters, weavers and coppersmiths as they might have long ago. The village weaver creates every bit of fabric worn by the villagers.

Also on site is a dungeon. What more could you want?

Photo by Kim Cool

The baptismal font of the Tiffany Chapel is at the side.
    Take I-75 north to Exit 261 (I-4). Travel east on I-4 to Exit
87 (Fairbanks). Turn right and get into the left lane. At Park
Avenue, turn left and travel four traffic lights to the museum
(445 Park Ave. S.) at the intersection of Park and Canton. Drive
past the building and turn left onto Cole Street. Park behind the
building. Call (407) 645-5311 or visit www.morsemuseum.org.

Charles Hosmer Morse Museum

More than a century after its debut at the 1893 World Exhibition in Chicago, one of the most spectacular creations of the famed New York glass studios, the Tiffany chapel was reassembled at Winter Park's Charles Hosmer Morse Museum after years in storage.

Moved from one site to another during its first half century, the chapel sustained a variety of injuries. It became an 800-square-foot puzzle, which conservator John Maseman and an army of colleagues took two years to reassemble. The worst damage occurred on the chapel's final trip. It was the bottom layer in a moving van, topped with furniture, resulting in a great deal of damage to the fragile glass sections of the chapel.

While the chapel is the most spectacular piece in the Morse Museum's collection of American art and design of the late 19th and early 20th centuries, there also are Tiffany windows, the Favrile Pottery and paintings of L.C. Tiffany, Tiffany lamps and lighting and domestic treasures for the public such as lustre glass tableware.

The artwork comprises the largest collection of Tiffany items under one roof, drawing visitors from around the world. The chapel is the biggest draw of all. It was planned to showcase both glass and bronze work by the Tiffany Studios when it was planned for the 1893 exhibition. There is a baptismal font in a side recess, tall glass mosaic-clad pillars, Tiffany chandeliers and the Field of Lilies window behind the baptismal. More than 1.4 million people, including my grandfather, visited the chapel at the Columbia Exposition in Chicago in 1893.

In addition to the Tiffany items, the museum has major collections of American art pottery and 19th and 20th century artwork. The Morse Museum is open Tuesday-Sunday.

Photo by Kim Cool

The entrance bridge to the Orlando Science Center is across from the second level of the museum's parking garage.

From Interstate 4, take Exit 85 (Princeton). Although the sign is to the left, stay to the right and follow the entrance road to the garage. Take the elevator to the walkway level and enjoy the view and you stroll above the road you were just on. For more information, call (407) 514-2110 or visit www.osc.org.

Orlando Science Center

Hands-on science centers can be fun, even on sunny days in Florida. The Orlando Science Center is one of the better ones.

Within its 50,000 square feet, visitors can be scientists for the day, view giant screen films and planetarium shows within the 300-seat Phillips CineDome, watch science demonstrations and live performances in the 250-seat Darden Adventure Theater, see stars and planets in the Crosby Observatory, and (most of all) experience a broad variety of hands-on opportunities on the center's four levels.

Park in the 600-car garage and enter the museum from its second level, walking across an enclosed glass walkway to the center's information desk and lobby.

Once you purchase your ticket and pick up your map, attack the center from the top down or bottom up or, check out the day's live shows and films and plan your tour around the showtimes. I like the top-down approach so I take the elevator to the fourth level, home of TechWorks, which focuses on the high-tech industries of Central Florida — computers, simulation, lasers, optics and entertainment technology like you find in the nearby theme parks as well as in your local movie theater. On the same level, in Micro World, you can see the region's only scanning electron microscope (SEM) available to the public. BodyZone explores the complex systems that work together within the human body. Nearby is a healthy living exhibit.

Stroll down the ramp to the third level, home of the Cosmic Tourist exhibit; to the second level for Science City and its physics park, the Darden Theater and visiting exhibits; and to the first level for Kids Town, the NatureWorks exhibit of Florida's diverse ecosystems and the CineDome, Planetarium, Club House and Cafe.

Photo By Kim Cool

The circa 1920 Polk Theatre in Lakeland features an interior design based on a Mediterranean village dominated by a townhouse setting with a starry ceiling. Elvis Presley appeared there in 1956. Other notables who appeared there were Sally Rand, Glenn Miller, Gene Autry and Tommy Dorsey. It began in the days of vaudeville and became a movie house. Today it shows films and hosts a performing arts series.

Performing Arts Venues

Dance

Central Florida Ballet Professional Company, www.centralfloridaballet.com, (407) 849-9948.

Theater

John and Rita Lowndes Shakespeare Center, home of the 324-seat Margeson Theater, the 118-seat Goldman Theater and the 936-seat Walt Disney Amphitheater at Lake Eola, all in Orlando-Loch Haven Park, www.shakespearefest.org, (407) 447-1700.

Mad Cow Theatre Company, 105 S. Magnolia Ave., Orlando, www.madcowtheatre.com, (407) 297-8788.

Orlando Repertory Theatre, 1001 Princeton St., Orlando, www.orlandorep.com, (407) 896-7365.

Orlando-UCF Shakespeare Festival, 812 East Rollins Street, Ste. 100, Orlando. www.shakespearefest.org, (407) 447-1701.

Polk Theatre, 127 S. Florida Ave., Lakeland. www.polktheatre.org, (863) 682-7553.

Theatre Winterhaven, 210 Cypress Gardens Blvd., Winter Haven, www.theatrewinterhaven.com, (863) 299-2672.

Photo by Kim Cool

Joker Marchant Stadium in Lakeland is the spring training home of the Detroit Tigers of the American League. It is considered one of the most beautiful parks in the Grapefruit League, and, since its recent remodeling, the second most difficult stadium in which to get player autographs. It remains one of the best in all baseball in which to catch balls.

Professional Sports

Arena Football
Orlando Predators, T.D. Waterhouse Centre, downtown
Orlando, www.orlandopredators.com, (407) 447-7337

Baseball - Spring Training parks
Atlanta Braves, Cracker Jack Stadium, Disney's Wide World of
Sports Complex, Lake Buena Vista,
http://atlanta.braves.mlb.com, (407) 939-GAME
Cleveland Indians, Chain of Lakes Park, 500 Cletus Allen Drive,
Winter Haven, http://cleveland.indians.mlb.com, (863) 293-3900
Detroit Tigers, Joker Marchant Stadium, 2301 Lakeland Hills
Blvd., http://detroit.tigers.mlb.com, (813) 287-8844
Houston Astros, Osceola County Stadium, 1000 Bill Beck Blvd.,
http://houstonastros.mlb.com, (407) 933-2520

Basketball
The Orlando Magic, TD Waterhouse Centre, Orlando, (800)
338-0005, (407) 896-2442
The Orlando Miracle, 1 Magic Place, Orlando (407) 916-9622

Jai-Alai
Orlando Jai-Alai, Highway 17-92 & SR 436, Fern Park,
Orlando, www.orlandojaialai.com, (407) 339-6221

Rodeo
Friday Night Rodeo, Kissimmee Sports Arena, 958 Hoagland,
Kissimmee, www.ksarodeo.com, (407) 933-0020

Photo courtesy of SeaWorld Orlando

Whale of a friendship — Shamu the killer whale spins SeaWorld animal trainer Caroline Gibbs during the Shamu Adventure show. SeaWorld trainers have worked for years to build a special relationship with these majestic animals.

From Orlando take Exit 72 off of Interstate 4. From Tampa and the south, take Exit 71 off of I-4. For general park information, call (407) 351-3600 or visit www.seaworld.com.

Sea World & Discovery Cove

SeaWorld Orlando may not be the oldest marine life park but it certainly has set the standard.

In addition to providing entertainment to millions of park visitors, it maintains animal rescue teams, on duty 24/7 to rescue injured, ill or stranded animals. The Orlando teams have saved more than 275 manatees, making the team the world's largest manatee rescue program. You can actually see rescued manatees in the Manatee Rescue attraction at the park.

SeaWorld provides daily shows featuring Shamu the 5-ton killer whale; Clyde and Seamore starring sea lions, otters and a walrus; a spectacular dolphin show; and Pets Ahoy, which features dogs, cats, birds, rats, skunks and pot-belly pigs, many rescued from animal shelters. At Clydesdale Hamlet, park guests can see the famous Budweiser Clydesdales as the eight-horse hitch is prepared for park parades. No longer do you have to visit St. Louis to see the Clydesdales.

Nor do you have to visit Key West to meet the creatures that inhabit the coral reefs of the Florida Keys. At SeaWorld Orlando, you can pet stingrays, feed and touch dolphins and see endangered sea turtles up close. Pacific Point Preserve duplicates the rocky northern Pacific coast and is home to sea lions and harbor seals. The Shark Encounter takes guests into an underwater tunnel where they are surrounded by eels, barracuda, venomous fish and sharks. In the Sharks Deep Dive, guests get close to more than 50 sharks, by swimming within a shark cage. There is an extra cost for this and for the marine mammal keeper experience. Other shows, thrill rides like Kraken, the only floorless coaster in Orlando, nine restaurants and more make SeaWorld a road-trip must.

Discovery Cove is a reservations only, oasis-like park across the street from SeaWorld. There you can swim with the dolphins in a more personal setting. Call (877) DISCOVERY.

Photo courtesy of SIlver Springs Park

One of the famous Silver Springs glass-bottomed boats floats past the Lighthouse ride. Boats offer passengers underwater views of the famous springs.

Located east of Ocala, on State Road 40/Silver Springs Boulevard, the park is open daily from 10 a.m.-5 p.m. From Interstate 75 take Exit 352 (S.R. 40). Travel east through downtown Ocala to Silver Springs Park. Call (352) 236-2121 for more information or visitwww.silversprings.com.

Silver Springs

With its famous glass-bottomed boats dating to 1878, Silver Springs was a theme park before the term was invented.

Below the boats is the crystal clear water that flows from seven artesian springs at the headwaters of the Silver Spring River. The largest spring, Mammoth Spring, pumps more than 550 million gallons of water from its sources each day, feeding the 74-degree Silver River that feeds into the Ocklawaha and St. Johns rivers, which lead into the Atlantic Ocean.

Today, Silver Springs is a 350-acre attraction including an accredited zoo, the Lost River Voyage through undeveloped wetlands, a jungle cruise down Fort King Waterway, Kids Ahoy Playland, Doolittle's Petting Zoo and a showcase that highlights the area's 10,000-year history.

Those who crave a little extra excitement will undoubtedly enjoy a ride aboard one of the zebra-striped Jeep Wranglers. They negotiate a 3-foot deep alligator pit while carrying passengers through the Florida jungle.

Park trainers present daily reptile shows featuring many of the park's native creatures, including a 110-pound freshwater alligator snapping turtle that has been performing in the park since 1937.

Sobek, a 16-foot long, 2,000-pound American crocodile is the show's largest performer.

The smallest performers at Silver Springs are the Egyptian fruit bats, tarantulas, scorpions and related insects. A "creature cam" allows guests to get up close and personal with the creatures without really getting up close and personal with them although there are some audience participation opportunities.

At the other extreme are performing pets from the humane society and Birds of the Rain Forest.

Special events are planned throughout the year.

Photo courtesy of Universal Orlando

Universal Orlando offers two theme parks, shopping and entertainment at City Walk plus three unique theme hotels. There is a unique VIP tour program that provides a personal theme park escort and red carpet treatment.

From Interstate I-4, take Exit 29-B, just south of Orlando and follow the signs to the park or resort of your choice at Universal Orlando. For more information, call (800) 711-0080 or visit www.universalorlando.com.

Universal Orlando

Size doesn't matter at Universal Orlando.

On less than two percent of the acreage of one of its competitors, Universal built three major resort hotels, two state-of-the-art theme parks and a 30-acre shopping and entertainment area.

The Lowe's managed hotels: the Portofino Bay Hotel, Hardrock Hotel and Royal Pacific Resort are destinations themselves. Swim, dine, shop or just kick back in style without ever leaving your resort. Height helps at the Portofino Bay Hotel where the extremely comfy beds also seem extremely high. That hotel looks postcard perfect and was ranked as one of the top 100 hotels in the U.S. by CondeNast travelers.
The Hard Rock has a Little Rock pool for the kids and the South Pacific has a Kul-Kul tower from Bali, orchids and a 12,000-square foot lagoon pool. All offer spas, daycare and concierge services.

CityWalk offers dining, dancing and drinking, primarily for the over-21 crowd. There are 12 restaurants, including Emeril's, Jimmy Buffet's Margaritaville and the Hard Rock Orlando, plus options for the over 21 crowd such as Pat O'Brien's, the New Orleans watering hole known for its specialty drink, the Hurricane.

When you do want to head into the parks for the ultimate thrill ride or to introduce the children to the Cat in the Hat, your resort key comes with a bonus — you to go to the head of the line on virtually all of the most popular rides and attractions, without the need for the Universal Express ride access system available to day guests of the parks.

Islands of Adventure offers Dueling Dragons on the Lost Continent, Seuss Landing, the dinosaurs of Jurassic Park and the Amazing Adventures of Spider-Man. The Dueling Dragons feature perilously intertwining paths of metal and dragon-shaped

Photo courtesy of Universal Orlando

**Universal Studios Revenge of the Mummy — the Ride
taps into riders' primal fears through immersion in a total multi-
sensory environment, the world's first psychological thrill ride,
placing riders in a terrifying underworld of ancient Egypt awash
in deadly curses, powerful forces of nature and ghostly creatures.
This is one of the many Universal Studios Orlando attractions
based on pop-culture icons and blockbuster films.**

racing cars, which furiously barrel towards and around each other at speeds close to 60 miles per hour, avoiding collision by mere inches. Even its queue is a record-breaker — the longest and most elaborate ride line in the world at 3,180 feet.

Yet the crown jewel of the Islands rides remains The Amazing Adventures of Spider-Man. It combines speed and simulators, utilizing technology from Universal's Back to the Future Ride and Terminator 2.

The Cat in the Hat and other Dr. Seuss characters come to life at Seuss Landing where you can dine at the Green Eggs and Ham Cafe. At Toon Lagoon, you can see what some of your favorite non-superhero characters do when they are not in the Sunday funnies. The super heroes are trapped on Marvel Super Hero Island. While there, ride the Incredible Hulk Coaster.

Newest and most amazing of the rides is "Revenge of the Mummy," which some think might even nudge Spider-Man off its pedestal. Billed as the "first psychological thrill ride," it offers the newest in theme-ride technology. The attraction features a fusion of cutting edge technology, high-speed coaster engineering and space-age robotics, which propels guests through special-effects-laden, ancient Egyptian catacombs.

Opened in 1990, Universal Studios was built with guidance from creative consultant Steven Spielberg. Its rides are based on movies such as "Twister," "Men in Black," "Shrek" and "Jaws."

Multi-day and annual passes are available. The whole complex is designed to be as hassle-free as possible for both day and overnight guests. The theme parks are side by side and all within a stroll or boat ride of the resorts and City Walk. There is a multi-level garage for one- day visitors.

For more information, call (888) UESCAPE (837-2273).

Photo by Kim Cool

Finding the mouse is easy.
 As you drive along Interstate 4, watch for this singular
high tension tower, opposite Celebration and south of Exit 62. If
heading east, you know you are very close to the Walt Disney
World Exit. If heading west — go back. WDW is big but not that
big. Use I-4 Exits 64-68 for the Magic Kingdom, Exits 67-68 for
Downtown Disney, Exit 67 for Epcot, Exit 65 for Epcot, MGM
Studios or Animal Kingdom and Exits 64 A and B for World
Drive, the original main entrance from Rte 92.

Walt Disney World

When the "World" came to Orlando in 1971, the state of Florida was forever changed. Walt Disney World was not the first theme park in Florida but, with nearly 30,000 acres and the most famous cartoon characters in history making daily appearances, Florida tourism would never again be the same.

Books have been written on the subject of Walt Disney's dream and to make the most of a multi-day adventure at WDW, you should consult such guide books as PassPorter Walt Disney World Resort® by Jennifer Watson and Dave Marx, any of the Birnbaum guidebooks to Walt Disney World or such speciality books as Hidden Mickeys by Steven M. Barrett. To do justice to the four main theme parks, the water parks, the hotels, miniature golf courses and Downtown Disney, plan to go there for several days. It won't be enough if you are a real Disney fan but you can see most of what is there, eat well and have a great time, with time left to plan your return.

If you have one day or less, it is even more important to do your homework. Determine what aspect of the World you absolutely must see and then do that, knowing you will have to return to see the rest of the "World" some other time.

Tickets to the World

There are new ticket offerings almost weekly. The best deals are for residents or Disney hotel guests, but many of the tickets have no expiration date (be sure to check on that when you make your purchase), so if you plan to ever return, don't be afraid to buy a multi-day park hopper pass that will allow you access to all the parks on a given day. I have some such tickets that are 10 years old and, given the price increases at WDW in that time period, those tickets are one of the best investments I have ever made.

Armed with park hopper tickets, it is quite possible to visit the four major Disney theme parks all in the same day and get a good overview of the "World."

If you just want to do the thrill rides, do that. Or, shop each park and just hit the classics like "It's a Small World" in the Magic Kingdom, "The Great Movie Ride" at Disney's MGM Studios, "Journey Into Imagination" and the new "Soarin'"at Epcot and "The Kilimanjaro Safaris" at Animal Kingdom.

Families with small children should ignore the above suggestions and concentrate on the Magic Kingdom. Walt Disney designed Disneyland as a park that he could enjoy with his then pre-teen daughter.

Since then parents have been dragging their youngsters to WDW in record numbers. You can see them in every park, tired parents pushing strollers containing sleeping or cranky children who are too young to really enjoy the park and the characters. But their parents or grandparents could not wait one more year to take junior to see that famous mouse.

Even though the tickets might cost more next year or the year after, I think the Disney parks are best enjoyed by children 10 and older. If you must ignore me, take your precocious 8-year olds. Your 2-year-old will not even remember the experience but you may have nightmares for years to come. Or, let Disney babysitters care for your littlest ones while you take the older children into the parks. Disney really is kid-friendly and there are plenty of Disney alternatives to pushing tired kids in strollers through the theme parks.

A good way to test the waters is to take the family to one of the Disney hotels for a character breakfast. The parents will get the pictures of Mickey or Goofy or Donald with their little ones and everyone will get a great meal. Call (407) WDW-DINE to make reservations for the character breakfasts anywhere at WDW. Some of the most popular ones are at the Fort Wilderness Resort, the Contemporary Hotel or the Grand Floridian.

Resort hotels

Staying at one of the Disney resorts is the way to enjoy the Magic with the least hassle. Resort guests can purchase length-of-stay park hopper tickets at a discount, have early access to the parks (parks alternate early access hours), can use any of the Disney transportation systems and enjoy other amenities such as free parking, package delivery to their hotel and more.

All the resorts offer disabled access and wheelchairs can be borrowed from every resort. Motorized wheelchairs can be rented only in the parks and are subject to availability.

Each of the resort hotels is different. They range from the moderately priced family-oriented Fort Wilderness Campground and the various All-Star Resorts to the Grand Floridian, which offers the ultimate in luxury accommodations and dining, including afternoon tea. Each is a destination itself so plan to spend time enjoying the ambiance of whichever resort you choose.

Dining at these hotels is another experience. Enjoy character breakfasts, lunches or dinners. Enjoy a South Pacific-style luau at the Polynesian or a most elegant formal dinner while being served by Victoria and Albert at Victoria and Albert's within the Grand Floridian. WDW's restaurants are worthy of a road trip themselves and one could easily spend a special day or more dining Disney style and then enjoying the grounds of one or more hotels and taking time to check out the various gift shops.

Don't forget to explore Downtown Disney and Disney Westside where you can shop until you drop, eat Wolfgang Puck's wood-fired pizzas and then catch a performance of Cirque du Soleil, if you can get tickets.

For more information, call (407) W-DISNEY or visit www.waltdisneyworld.com

Kim Cool

Part II
Out and about
Tampa/St. Pete
& Clearwater

Photo courtesy of Busch Gardens Tampa Bay

Photo by Kim Cool

Located at Berth 271, 705 Channelside Drive, Tampa,
behind the Florida Aquarium. Take Interstate 275 take Exit 44
(Downtown West, Ashley, Scott and Tampa streets). Follow signs
to aquarium and turn left on Channelside Drive. Park next to the
ship or in the Tampa Port Authority Garage off 12th Street. Call
(813) 228-8766, for information or visitwww.americanvictory.org.

American Victory

Saved by love, sweat, some $4 million and an act of Congress, the Victory ship, "American Victory," sails again, more than 50 years after its launching in California, on June 20, 1945.

Now docked in Tampa, behind the aquarium, the 455-foot long ship used by Merchant Mariners could move through the water at a speedy 17 knots.

Able to outrun German and Japanese subs, Victory ships were manned by some 60 civilian volunteers and powered by steam turbine engines. By the Vietnam era, the ship was manned by less than half that number.

"Merchant Mariners suffered the greatest loss of life, one of 26 during World War II," Victory spokesman Tim Teahan said. The ships, including this one now based in Tampa, were used in three wars. Two of the ships were named for Florida colleges — Rollins and Stetson.

Kept in mothballs for much of its life, the American Victory was pulled out in 1985 for a test to see how quickly it could be reactivated. Because it was cleaned up and actually sailed for 24 hours before going back in the reserve fleet, this ship was in relatively good shape when delivered to Tampa for its new career as a tourist draw. It is just the third ship of its class to be restored, and the only one on the East coast. A restored Liberty ship is in Baltimore.

Volunteers donated labor, paint, money and in-kind services to reactivate the ship as a floating museum. In addition to occasional cruises, the ship is the site of weddings, private parties and special Maritime observances.

Tours, quarterly sails and occasional dramatic productions are offered as restoration work continues on the historic ship.

Photo opportunities abound and T-shirts and other souvenirs can be purchased in the ship's gift shop.

Photo courtesy of Busch Gardens Tampa Bay
Riders on Montu at Busch Gardens Tampa Bay.
Take Interstate 75 to Exit 33 (Busch Boulevard) Turn left on Busch Boulevard and then left on McKinley Drive. The park is on the left. For more information, visit www.buschgardens.com or call (800) 42-KUMBA.

Busch Gardens Tampa Bay

At the original Busch attraction in Tampa Bay, the giant escalator leading to the factory tour was the biggest thrill ride.

Today, Busch Gardens Tampa Bay has grown into one of the country's premier "white knuckle ride" theme parks. The escalator is longgone, replaced by thrill rides that soar to far greater heights. There is live entertainment, a major zoological park (the first free-range habitat for herds of animals in the U.S.) and an ice rink, which hosts regular shows.

Coaster buffs rank Kumba and Montu among the top steel roller coasters in the world. For the purists, there is Gwazi, a wooden double racing coaster, built from 1.25 million board feet of lumber. Takes me back to my childhood in Cleveland, Ohio, where I would ride the wooden racing coaster at the old Euclid Beach Park. It was fast but probably not as fast as Gwazi, which reaches speeds of more than 50 miles per hour. Six flybys add to the excitement. The coasters are the park's third generation of rides, following the original monorail above the herds of animals and the Stanley Falls log flume ride of the 1970s. SheiKra began inducing screams in 2005 at Florida's tallest coaster at 200 feet. It is the new centerpiece in Stanleyville.

For visitors who prefer to keep their feet planted on the ground, the park has expanded its entertainment venues as rapidly as its assortment of coasters.

TV shows have been regularly filmed there. Water and kiddy rides round out the offerings of this family-oriented tourist attraction.

A variety of one-day and annual passes are available, including multi-park deals that include admission to Sea World Florida, Adventure Island Water Park, Universal Studios and Universal Studios Islands of Adventure.

For recorded information, call (813) 987-5082.

Photo by Kim Cool

Salvador Dali's life and work are well represented in a unique collection assembled by his most ardent fans.

The museum is at 1000 Third St., St. Petersburg. Take Interstate 275 to Exit 9 and follow I-175 East signs to Fourth Street South. Go right on Fourth Street South to 11th Avenue South, then left to Third Street South for the museum and parking area. For information visit www.salvadordalimuseum.org or call (800) 442-3254.

Salvador Dali Museum

Salvador Dali painted more than melted clocks but I had to move to Florida to learn about his extraordinary training and talent.

Only in Florida did I visit the museum that had been nearly in my backyard when I lived in Shaker Heights Ohio, on the east side of Cleveland. Funded by the A. Reynolds Morse family of Beachwood, an adjacent suburb, the Dali Museum never got my patronage, which was my loss.

Some people may find it hard to take seriously a man who grew a handlebar mustache in the hopes of attracting flies, but art experts acknowledge that Dali was a fine technician as well as a creative artist.

To see for yourself, you need only spend a few hours at his St. Petersburg museum as I finally did.

Classically trained, the Spanish Surrealist worked in many media. Multiple examples of each are in St. Petersburg.

Within the collection are more than 100 watercolors and drawings, 1,300 graphics, posters, photographs, sculptures, objets d'art, an archival library on Dali and Surrealism and several monumental works, including at least one with what appear to be marching flies.

When Dali turned from surrealism to classicism, he created 19 wall-sized canvases, depicting scientific, historical or religious themes. One of the best known of these is "The Discovery of America by Christopher Columbus." It is in the museum's collection.

The artist was a superb draftsman. His painting technique was brilliant.

The Morse collection's first Dali painting was "Daddy Longlegs of the Evening - Hopel," purchased in 1943, in honor of their first wedding anniversary.

45

Photo by Kim Cool

The Florida Aquarium is open daily from 9:30 a.m.-5 p.m. It is closed on Thanksgiving and Christmas.

Take Interstate 4 to the 22nd Street Exit and follow the signs to the aquarium. You will turn right on State Road 60, which will turn into Channelside Drive. The aquarium is located at 701 Channelside Drive, Tampa, close to the Ice Palace. Parking garages offer plenty of room. For more information, visit flaquarium.netcall (813) 273-9583.

Florida Aquarium

Fish stories abound at the Florida Aquarium, which also is home to a coastal ecosystem learning center. The parking lot is a stormwater management experiment.

Within the multi-storied building on Channelside Drive one can see albino alligators, full-grown sharks, wetland areas, frightful exhibits that contain such creatures as a reticulated python, a yellow anaconda, vultures and vampire bats.

Thousands of fish can be seen in aquariums that rise from floor to ceiling. Seeing it all is simple. Visitors ride an escalator to the top and then walk slowly back to the lower level on a gently inclined path. Along the way it is virtually impossible not to soak up a lot of environmental knowledge.

At the 5,000-gallon touch pool, you can actually pet a shark or a ray — if you want to.

Florida's water story is more than a parking lot story. Within the building one sees the springs where rain is filtered through a limestone aquifer, feeding clear streams that are home to mergansers who thrive on the lush vegetation. So do nearly 50 juvenile American alligators found in the same marsh grasses. That is what this aquarium is all about — Florida habitats above and below water. Fish and wildlife appropriate to Florida's many native habitats are here, sharing space with appropriate flora and fauna.

Most spectacular of all the exhibits is the Florida Coral Reefs Gallery, which simulates a 60-foot dive from shallow-water reefs to deeper darker waters containing an artificial reef with more than 1,450 reef residents — 65 Florida native species.

Finally at the bottom, one is mesmerized by the 43-foot wide, 14-foot tall panoramic window in which sunlight from the surface makes silhouettes of coral colonies which are framed by schools of brightly colored fishes, sharks and rays.

47

Photo by Kim Cool

Take Interstate 275 to Exit 23A (I-375 East). Follow I-375 East signs to Fourth Street North. Turn right onto Fifth Street and travel four blocks south. The museum is immediately on the right after you cross Central Avenue. Parking is free in the lot on the north side of the museum. Metered parking is available on the street during the day. Parking is free on Sundays. For more information, visit www.floridaholocaustmuseum.org or call (800) 960-7448.

Florida Holocaust Museum

All day and all night, the stories of the Holocaust are told. Taped interviews with victims of those black days are played and replayed, never stopping. Other voices ooze out of the pictures on the walls. Silently poignant, the haunting pictures of the people who endured those dark years tell the story in another way.

In the museum's atrium, a box car, 113 0695-5 (5), resting on tracks from Treblinka, tells another version of one of the most horrific times in the history of man. During the Holocaust when millions of Jews and those thought sympathetic to Jews were systematically exterminated, this car carried as many as 100 men, women and children to their deaths in the camps. Almost too grisly to even think about is the likely fate of a young child whose ring was found in the door track of this box car when it was being cleaned and prepared to be installed in the museum. Like the tapes and the photos, the ring tells a tale.

Permanent exhibits in the museum depict the people who lived in Eastern Europe, before, during and after World War II. An overview of the entire museum and its story can be seen in the 40-seat auditorium on the first floor. Other areas of the museum tell the story of the Nazi rise to power, Kristallnacht, the persecution of Jews, the Holocaust and the birth of the state of Israel. Signage embellishes the story, as do the witness testimonies that run continuously.

The museum chapel offers a place where one can sit silently, considering and absorbing what is within this hallowed place. There are three floors of exhibits, a library and meeting space.

Special shows throughout the year are chosen for their relevance to the museum's message that one person can make a difference. If you go to this museum, perhaps that one person will be you.

Photo by Kim Cool

The Florida International Museum was planning a move to a
new home as this book was being printed. Above is the 100
Second Street North location. The new location was scheduled to
open in the fall of 2005 at 244 Second Avenue North.

From Interstate 275, take Exit 23 or 23A (I-375 East)
Turn right and go two blocks to Second Avenue North. Turn left.
The parking garage will be to the right. For more information,
visit www.floridamuseum.org or call (727) 822-3693.

Florida International Museum

It was an especially sunny day in Florida when the famous Smithsonian Institution spread its wings and landed in St. Petersburg, with a major exhibition about the late President John F. Kennedy at the Florida International Museum.

That was back in 1995.

In the ensuing years, the museum has hosted Splendors of Ancient Egypt, Treasures of the Tsars, the Titanic and even Lady Diana, the latter a show directly from the Spencer family estate Althorp in England.

While many items within the Kennedy exhibit became the basis for the museum's permanent collection, it is the big traveling exhibits mentioned above that bring thousands of visitors to its doors.

The museum's mission is to present diverse national and international themed exhibits focusing on history.

The Cuban Missile Crisis is a permanent 10,000-square-foot exhibition that allows visitors to relive the early 1960s in several retro rooms and a circa 1960s living room in which Kennedy's speech from October 1962 is replayed on an old TV set.

The FIM has been an affiliate museum of the Smithsonian Institution since 1999.

Plan to spend an average of two hours in the museum and additional time in the museum's gift shop, which always has a wonderful selection of items themed to the current show as well as items from earlier showings.

Like other attractions in the downtown St. Petersburg area, the museum is on the line of the The Looper, the trolley service that connects the major sites in downtown St. Petersburg.

An education guide is available to assist teachers in preparing for school trips. The museum's parking garage is on Second Avenue North.

Photo by Kim Cool

Flowers frame the Gulf Coast Museum of Art.

Take Interstate 275 to Exit 16 (Clearwater-Largo) and travel that road to SR 688 (Ulmerton Road. Travel West on Ulmerton, approximately 12 miles to 12211 Walsingham Road. Turn left.

To learn more about the museum, visit www.gulfcoastmuseum.org or call (727) 518--6833.

Gulf Coast Museum of Art

Early Florida women's clubs spawned libraries, theaters and, in Largo, the Gulf Coast Museum of Art. The GCMA began in the 1930s as the art section of the Clearwater Women's Club, and was incorporated as a museum in 1936, making it one of the oldest museums in the state.

Relocated to its present site in Pinewood Cultural Park in 1947, the museum concentrates its efforts on assembling a permanent collection of Florida and American contemporary art and crafts. Its focus is on works from the 12 southeastern states. There is a strong post-modern tendency and the use of visual metaphors to communicate ideas and stimulate dialog.

Located on the yet-to-be completed museum campus are nine permanent collection galleries, a teaching auditorium, museum store and two studio buildings for the use of artists. Yet to come are additional classrooms, more studio space, space for artists in residence and a restaurant.

Pinewood Cultural Park, adjacent to Heritage Village, contains the Florida Botanical Gardens, which offer inspiration to visiting and resident artist as well as visitors to the 250-acre site. Sculptures on the grounds are part of the art museum collection.

Heritage Village is a 21-acre living history museum that relates the history of Pinellas County.

In addition to its permanent collection, the museum regularly hosts several visiting exhibitions and an annual juried show featuring the work of its instructors and students.

Educational programs include classes for adults and children, panel discussions, lectures, seminars, workshops and video programs. After school classes for children are held during the school year. A summer youth camp is held annually.

The museum is accredited by the American Association of Museums.

Photo courtesy of the Lowery Park Zoo

Africa here we come.

Take Interstate 75 to Exit 228 (I-275 North). There will be a $1 toll on the Skyway Bridge. Travel north on I-275 to Exit 48 (Sligh Ave.) Stay to the left on the exit ramp. Turn left onto Sligh. The zoo will be on the right, approximately one mile from the I-275 exit. For more information, visit www.lowryparkzoo.com or call (813) 935-8552.

Lowry Park Zoo

A zoo's who of the creatures to be found at the Lowry Park Zoo in Tampa Bay would include 1,600 animals that represent more than 330 species. This 41-acre zoological park is considered the number one family-friendly zoo in the United States. It is the Tampa Bay region's only zoological garden and a center for education and endangered species conservation.

Its natural outdoor exhibits offer habitats for animals from Florida and animals from areas with similar habitats. Moats and gullies separate animals housed in settings as much like their native habitats as possible rather than in cages.

Designed for children of all ages, the zoo has a manatee statue-enhanced fountain near the entrance, which is a sure lure for little zoo visitors, and, on a hot Florida day, mighty tempting to adults.

At Lorikeet Landing, a free-flight aviary attraction, the brightly colored birds will land on you and eat nectar out of small cups that you may purchase.

In the zoo's Africa area you can feed giraffes, getting eye-to-eye with the world's tallest animal. The only other place in the zoo where you can feed the inhabitants is the pond at Alice Springs Kookaburra Windmill. There you can feed the koi fish. The pond is near Wallaroo station, the Australia-themed children's zoo in a zoo, where children can pet kangaroos, wallabies and goats, ride a horse or ride through a herd of sheep in a "ute." Feeding yourself is easy here, with snack bars and restaurants in several locations.

At Stingray Bay pet the stingrays, (the barbs have been removed) and then look, but don't touch, the Komodo Dragon from Indonesia — not a people-friendly creature like the manatees found in the Manatee Amphitheater

An eco boat tour is one of the newer attractions. So are the five white rhinos and the safari school in Africa, Phase II.

Photo by Kim Cool

The entrance to the parking lot is to the right of the tower, near the IMAX Dome.

Take Interstate 75 to Exit 265 (Fowler Avenue). Follow the signs to MOSI, which is at 4801 E. Fowler Ave. For more information, visit www.mosi.org or call (813) 987-6300.

MOSI (Museum of Science & Industry

At the Museum of Science and Industry (MOSI) in Tampa you can feed your mind and do a little bungee jumping as well. MOSI is the largest science center in the southeastern United States, with more than 450 hands-on activities available on its three levels.

Two life-size dinosaur skeletons greet visitors. Each skeleton is 75 feet long and towers more than three stories above ground level. From dinosaurs to the IMAX Dome Theater, there is more than enough to keep you busy for at least four hours at this museum. And then you can go outside and jump on the trampolines while attached to bungee harnesses.

Science exhibits demonstrate the way lightning can start fires and how a tornado begins.

The Tower of Trash was planned to make you think about the environment and man's contributions.

On the next level you can learn about the human body and on the third level, learn about the universe as well as planet Earth and its place in the solar system.

Be sure to take time for an IMAX film, which is projected on to the 10,500-square-foot dome-shaped screen. A six channel, multi-speaker sound system enhances the film and you feel as though you are right in the middle of the action.

MOSI is home to Tampa's only planetarium with shows scheduled throughout the day and on weekends. "Star parties" are held on Saturday evenings.

Outside visitors can experience the force of hurricane winds in the Gulf Coast Hurricane. Sit in this booth and experience the force of 75 mph winds.

Have a drink and snack in MOSI's Cafe before you make your last stop, the Science Store, to purchase a souvenir of your visit.

Photo by Kim Cool

This classic Palladian building houses the Museum of Fine Arts on the waterfront in downtown St. Petersburg.

Take Interstate 275 Exit 23-A or 23 (I-375) which becomes 4th Avenue North. Continue until the road ends at Beach Drive. Turn right for one and one-half blocks. The museum is at 255 Beach Drive NE. There is a parking lot just north of the museum. For more information, visit www.fine-arts.org or call (727)896-2667.

Museum of Fine Arts

In a Palladian-styled building near St. Petersburg's waterfront is a specialty museum that containing works by Georgia O'Keefe, Paul Cezanne, Berthe Morisot, Claude Monet and Frank Stella, and also has been known to offer special shows curated by its staff, in conjunction with some of the finest museums in the world.

Its location near the Renaissance Vinoy and charming bayfront shops makes it an especially fine road-trip destination.

Founder Margaret Acheson Stuart (1896-1980)hoped to amass a well-rounded art collection that would be an historical presentation of the ages even though so many major works by the great masters already were in permanent collections here and abroad. She and her followers succeeded admirably. Today's museum contains items from Cycladic sculpture of the third millennium B.C. to masterpieces of impressionism.

Recent special exhibits include an incredible show created with the help of glass artist Dale Chihuly. He paired his work to items in the museum's permanent collection. A Monet show, curated in-house brought some of the finest Monet works to St. Petersburg before traveling to other museums.

Even the building itself is an important work. It was designed by the Palm Beach architectural firm of John L. Volk and is reminiscent of magnificent villas of Venice. There is a Spanish influence in the shaded walkways balanced by the warmth of red barrel tiles on the roof.

The interior's 24-foot ceilings in the entrance lobby, a grand lobby and reception area were especially useful for the Chihuly show. Galleries vary in their proportions and are more like rooms in a private home. Visitor parking is in a lot to the north of the museum and along Beach and Bayshore drives.

Photo courtesy of the Tampa Bay Performing Arts Center

The Tampa Bay Performing Arts Center, the largest such center in the southeast, hosts world-class entertainment in five theaters. Dine in its upscale restaurant and purchase souvenirs of the show in its gift shop. For tickets and information, call (800) 955-1045 or (813) 229-7827 or visit TBPAC.org. Take Exit 44 from Interstate 275.

Performing Arts Venues

Acorn Theatre, 14313 Capitol Drive, Tampa, (813) 363-8562.

American Stage, 211 Third Street South, St. Petersburg, (727) 823-7529

Bayfront Center Arena/Mahaffey Theater, 400 S. First Street, St. Petersburg, www.stpete.org/bayfront.htm, (727) 892-5796.

Bits 'n Pieces Puppet Theater, 12904 Tom Gallagher Road, Plant City, (813) 659-0659

Carrolwood Players, 4331 Gunn Highway, Tampa, (813) 265-4000.

Falk Theater, 428 W. Kennedy Blvd., Tampa, (727) 866-1973

Francis Wilson Playhouse, 302 Seminole St., Clearwater, www.franciswilsonplayhouse.org, (727) 446-1360

Gorilla Theatre Company, 4419 N. Hubert Ave., Tampa, www.gorillatheatre.com, (813) 879-2914

Mark Two Dinner Theatre, 3376 Edgewater Drive, Orlando, (407) 843-6275 or (800) 726-6275

Off Center Theater, within Tampa Bay Performing Arts Center, Tampa, (813) 222-1087

Plant City Community Theater, Plant City, (813) 707-8100.

Royalty Theatre, 405 Cleveland St., Clearwater, (727) 447-2277

Ruth Eckerd Hall, 1111 McMullen Booth Road, Clearwater, www.ruthereckerdhall, (727) 791-7400

Sleuths Mystery Dinner Shows, 7508 Universal Blvd., Orlando, www.sleuths.com, (407) 363-1985 or (800) 393-1985

St. Petersburg Little Theater, 4025 31st Street South, St. Petersburg, (727) 866-1973

Stageworks Theater Company, 120 Adriatic Ave., Tampa, (813) 251-8954

Tampa Bay Performing Arts Center, 1010 North MacInnes Place, Tampa, www.tampacenter.com, (813) 229-7827

West Coast Players, Our Lady of Lourdes Church, San Salvador, Dunedin, (727) 773-0411

Photo courtesy of the Strawberry Festival.
Top your strawberries with plenty of whipped cream.
Take Interstate 4 to Exit 10 (Branch Forbes Road) or Exit
11 (Thonotosassa Road) and follow the signs to the festival
grounds. For more information about the festival, visit
www.flstrawberryfestival.com or call (813) 752-9194.

Plant City Strawberry Festival

It's the berries.

When the strawberry fields ripen in late February or early March each winter, the world beats a path to the Plant City Fairground, site of the annual Strawberry Festival.

Less than 30 minutes from the Interstate, the annual festival is like a fair but tastier. At this one, you can have your cake topped with berries and whipped cream as you check out the entertainment, carnival rides, poultry shows, rabbit shows, beef shows, handicrafts and at least three parades.

Bring your appetite and your wallet so you can overdose on the berries (especially the make-your-own shortcake) and take home a carload of the "berry" finest souvenirs.

Pick as many berries as your car will hold. Take home some plants. Learn the proper way to dip strawberries in chocolate and other toppings. Enjoy some bluegrass or Glen Campbell or some other famous personality in concert. For one sweet day, forget about calories.

At just 97 calories for a cup and one half, strawberry calories don't add up to much anyway and one cup provides an entire day's requirement of vitamin C. If you really must count those pesky calories, skimp on the shortcakes and whipped cream and go heavy on the reason for the festival. A festival spokesman said the average person consumes 3.1 pounds of strawberries annually. You might be able to do that in a day at this event. Or cool off with strawberry ice cream as you sit back and enjoy one of the festival's parades in Plant City.

The city was named for railroad baron Henry B. Plant after he connected the South Florida Railroad to the north at what was then called Hichipuckassa.

The Plant City Union Depot, built in 1909, on East North Drane Street is a legacy of those days. So are the strawberries.

Photo by Kim Cool

Built in 1891 by Henry Bradley Plant, the former Tampa Bay Hotel is now home to the Henry B. Plant Museum.

From Interstate 75, take Exit 256 (the Crosstown Expressway Toll Road) toward Tampa. Merge on to the South Crosstown Expressway (SR 618 West - some portions are toll). Take Exit 5 toward Hyde Park Avenue/Davis Islands. Turn right on to South Plant Avenue and then left onto West John F. Kennedy Boulevard (SR 60/685) to 401 W. Kennedy Blvd.

For more information, visit www.plantmuseum.com or call (813) 254-1891.

Henry B. Plant Museum

Capped by silvery minarets on its many towers, the Tampa Bay Hotel welcomed its turn-of-the century visitors. Not merely a hotel, it was a resort destination planned by its builder Henry B. Plant as a destination for customers of his railroad.

Plant was to the West Coast of Florida what Henry Flagler was to the East Coast. Plant's railroad empire paved the way for the development of commerce and tourism on Florida's west coast. His hotel has been called a Turkish and Moorish fantasy of minarets, domes, cupolas, gingerbread trimmed arches and rambling verandas. Still the most recognizable building in the city, it once was the place to see and to be seen.

With 500 hotel rooms, public rooms and verandas, it was, and is, enormous. Today, it is a landmark as well as a destination for railroad buffs and others who come to the museum to learn about the hotel's gilded age, the history of that era and about Plant. The railroad man made his fortune buying up distressed southern railroads at the end of the Civil War. With help from several northern capitalists, including Henry Flagler, he set up a holding company that repaired and extended several rail lines, to provide continuous service in Florida, and improved connections to the north.

Tampa, a mere village at the time, was his southern terminus and the home of his resort hotel. A streetcar brought guests to the hotel from the train station.

Plant owned 14 railroads, several steamship companies, the Tampa Bay Hotel and the largest wood structure in Florida, Belleview Biltmore Hotel in neighboring Clearwater. The two hotels are the only remaining structures from Plant's hotel chain. Plant's train station was replaced by the Tampa Union Station at 601 N. Nebraska Ave., in 1912, 13 years after his death. That building was reopened in 1998 for Amtrak.

Photo by Kim Cool
**Brighthouse Field in Clearwater is the new home of the
minor league Clearwater Threshers and the spring training
home of the Philadelphia Phillies of the National League.**

Professional Sports

Arena Football
Tampa Bay Storm, St. Pete Times Forum, 401 Channelside, Tampa, www.tampabaystorm.com, (813) 276-7300

Baseball - Spring Training parks
New York Yankees, Legends Field, 1 Steinbrenner Drive, Tampa, http://newyork.yankees.mlb.com, (813) 879-2244
Philadelphia Phillies, Brighthouse Field, 601 Old Coachman Road, Clearwater, http://philadelphia.phillies.mlb.com, (727) 442-8496
Tampa Bay Devil Rays, Progress Energy Park, 230 First Street S., St. Petersburg, http://tampabay.devilrays.mlb.com, (727) 825-3250
Toronto Blue Jays, Dunedin Stadium, 373 Douglas Ave., Dunedin, http://toronto.bluejays.mlb.com, (727) 133-0429

Professional Football
Tampa Bay Buccaneers, Raymond James Stadium, 4201 North Dale Mabry, Tampa, www.buccaneers.com, (813) 879-BUCS

Professional Hockey
Tampa Bay Lightning, St. Pete Times Forum, 401 Channelside, Tampa, www.tampabaylightning.com, (813)229-BOLT

Photo by Kim Cool

St. Petersburg's Sunken Gardens has many cascading pools. Take Interstate 275 to Exit 23A (I-375) East which feeds into Fourth Street North. Turn left. The gardens will be on your right, between 17th and 18th streets. There is ample free parking. For more information, visit www.stpete.org/sunken.htm or call (727) 551-3100.

Sunken Gardens

In its second century Historic Sunken Gardens in north St. Petersburg is a spectacular 4-acre tropical garden filled with giant bougainvillaea and other specimen flowers plus soothing water features. Saved by the city, the garden is a renovation work in progress. It shares its new entrance with the adjacent Exploreum children's museum.

The city's mission is to "preserve and enhance Historic Sunken Gardens and to provide enjoyment and unique opportunities for the study of a tropical forest through diverse educational and cultural experiences."

From public market to Coca Cola® bottling plant to the world's largest gift shop, the garden's main building ushers visitors into a verdant jungle garden that is 10-15 feet below street level, with a mile of garden paths that meander through its four acre site. The largest bougainvillaea plants I had ever seen frame the back wall of the garden, shielding it from the residential neighborhood just beyond the fence, yet miles away.

Plants and flowers fill or decorate former animal cages, which are no longer used. Only a few token birds — mainly Chilean flamingoes — remain from the early zoological residents of the original Sunken Gardens. Their shrimp food-based diet helps them to maintain their bright pink color that coordinates so well with the giant bougainvillaea plants. They are usually to be found next to the large koi fish pond rather than another pond housing a giant snapping turtle.

Appropriate to the age of the gardens are several staghorn ferns that measure at least four feet in diameter. Specimen plants include Royal Palms, a Queen Sago nearly 12 feet tall, crotons in every color, impatiens, a loquat tree laden with fruit and Traveler Palm trees.

Bring your camera.

Photo by Kim Cool

Early cigar workers lived in houses such as these in Ybor City, Tampa.

From Interstate 75, take Exit 261 (I-4) west toward Tampa. Take Exit 1 from I-4 and cross the first traffic light at 22nd Street. Turn left (south) on 21st Street. Seventh Avenue is six blocks south of the Interstate. Limited parking is available on Seventh Avenue. Maps are available in most stores and parking lots are located throughout Ybor. For more information, visit www.ybor.org or call (813) 248-3712.

Ybor City

When Don Vincente Martinez Ybor moved from Key West to Tampa in 1886, he was followed by some 20,000 migrant workers, mostly from Cuba.

They lived side by side in small houses and worked side by side in large cigar factories. As they worked they would learn about the day's events from readers who were hired to read to the workers. A shopping mall filled with quirky antique stores has replaced the largest of the cigar factories but the old Ferlita Bakery building and the 1905 building housing the famous Columbia restaurant remain. The bakery, near the corner of Ninth Avenue and 19th Street, now houses the Ybor City State Museum. Walking tours are given on most days and a small ornamental garden is next to the museum. On weekends there is a small market across the street. The Columbia Restaurant is two blocks away near the corner of Seventh Avenue and 19th Street. Try the 1905 salad or its famous bean soup.

On weekend evenings, most of the action takes place on Seventh Avenue, from 19th to 14th Street (Avenida Republica de Cuba.) There are costume shops, tattoo parlors, night clubs, bars and more bars, plus a few cigar shops. During the daylight hours, you can still see cigars being hand-rolled in some of those shops as well as in the State Museum.

At the Muvica 20, you can catch the latest movies and then shop until you drop in any of several stores in the area of the Pleasuredome.

The Tampa Trolley is a 2.4-mile streetcar system that connects Ybor City via 10 stops to Tampa's Channel District via downtown Tampa's central business district. There are four stops in Ybor City. Or, spend time on a Duck Adventure.

When Halloween comes to the U.S. Guavaween, a family funfest, comes to Ybor City. Check with Ticketmaster.

Kim Cool

Part III
Check out the
Culture Coast

Photo courtesy of Crowley Museum & Nature Center

While walking the lengthy boardwalk at Crowley Museum & Nature Center, one can get a sense of Florida wilderness as it might have been for the early settlers in the area.

Take Interstate 75 to Exit 210 (Fruitville Road - SR 780). Travel east for 11 miles to Myakka Road. Turn right. Travel 2.5 miles to the Crowley entrance. Myakka Road twists and turns so watch carefully for the sign on your left. For more information, visit www.crowleymuseumnaturectr.org or call (941) 322-1000.

Crowley Museum & Nature Center

Located on 190 acres of native land adjacent to the Myakka River is a special place that is part park and part history center.

While meandering along the winding boardwalk above the Maple Branch Swamp and Tatum Sawgrass Marsh, visitors can see what this area of Sarasota County and much of Florida looked like when the first homesteaders arrived sometime after 1850. The difference is that Crowley visitors do not have to slice their way through miles of saw palmetto, which is aptly named because it will cut people to ribbons should they venture too close. From the top of the observation tower there are breathtaking views of the Myakka River.

In the pioneer history area of Crowley, there is a one-room homestead cabin, a working blacksmith shop, a museum filled with artifacts from pioneer days, a working sugar cane mill and a restored 1892 "Cracker" house. The Tatum Ridge Schoolhouse, built in 1905, is the oldest surviving schoolhouse in Sarasota County. In need of restoration, the building was moved to Crowley in 2000. Time and money are needed.

Many but not all of the trails at Crowley are handicap accessible. Self-guided tours allow visitors to stroll at their own pace, and picnic tables are available for those visitors who want to make a day of it and enjoy lunch in the shade of one of the magnificent old oak trees at the center.

Annual events include a folk music festival in the fall and Pioneer Days in early December.

Most Saturday mornings, there will be some sort of education program. Learn about container gardening, alligators, native plants, birds and other wildlife from experts.

Crowley is generally open from 10 a.m.-4 p.m. from Tuesday-Sunday during the winter tourist season and on fewer days during the summer months. It is best to call first.

Photo by Kim Cool

Live green with help from Florida House.
Florida House Learning Center is at 4600 Beneva Road South at Proctor in Sarasota.
From Interstate 75, take Exit 210 (Fruitville) west to Beneva Road. Go north on Beneva to Proctor. Florida House is on the northeast corner. Admission is free. For more information, including hours, visit http://sarasotaextension.ufl.edu/FHLC/fla-house.html or call (941) 316-1200.

Florida House Learning Center

Live greener and more efficiently in SW Florida with a lot of help from the Florida House Learning Center in Sarasota.

The center is a 2,375-square-foot demonstration house and garden that is operated by the University of Florida's Cooperative Extension Service. The house is filled with ideas to help homeowners cut utility bills, reduce maintenance chores, while living greener and healthier. Built in 1994, it was the first such demonstration house in the United States.

The energy-efficient house is a showcase for earth-friendly building and landscape products and practices. Minimizing the need for air conditioning is a cupola, which draws hot air up and out of the house while providing extra light during the day. One room is lit during the day by a solar tube and wide porches shade windows to keep the heat out of the house. Another room is powered by solar tubing that delivers power to a bank of batteries that store energy for evening use.

Cooperative Extension service agents, with help from a team of master gardeners, maintain the house and share building and gardening tips with visitors.

The gardeners have designed a landscape that not only looks good but needs the least possible water and maintenance. Water collected in a cistern supplies the water for the garden, which includes fruit trees and edible plants like pineapples. A new Zen-like sand garden that is changed daily by visitors has become one of the most popular additions to the Florida Yard.

Florida House is a healthy house built with non- and least-toxic materials. Decking is made of recycled plastic that will not rot, rust or mildew. Wood floors are made from replenishable materials like cork and bamboo.

Free public programs are given each Tuesday at 1 p.m. throughout most of the year. Open Tuesday-Saturday. Call first.

Photo by Kim Cool

A picnic area with a pavilion is at the rear of the Gamble Mansion.

From Interstate 75, travel west on U.S. 301 from Exit 224 to 3708 Patten Ave. The Gamble Plantation State Historic Site will be on your right. For more information, call (941) 723-4536.

Gamble Mansion

Civil War reenactments are part of the drill at Bradenton's Gamble Mansion.

Clad in handmade garments like their ancestors might have worn 150 years ago, history buffs set up camp and reenact battles and other events of those long ago days.

They generally gather on the first Friday of each month to set up camp for an authentic Civil War Reenactment. It is open to the public the next day.

In early March, during the annual open house held at the Gamble Plantation, visitors to the state historic site can tour the only remaining ante-bellum mansion in South Florida. See actors in period costumes, listen to authentic music of the period, see folk and craft demonstrations and spend a delightful afternoon going back in time to the 1850s.

Open houses feature embroiderers, basket makers, demonstrations by members of the local herb society, and guided tours of the Gamble Mansion plantation house.

The plantation house is the oldest building in Manatee County. It was built by Major Robert Gamble, a veteran of the Second Seminole War which ended in 1842, opening the area for settlement. Gamble was a planter who was attracted to the area by its potential for large-scale cultivation of sugar. Financed by his father, he eventually had a 3,450-acre plantation with 1,500 acres under cultivation, producing 1,500 barrels of sugar per year. The 10-room manor house was constructed by the same slaves who tended the sugar fields.

In 1856, Gamble sold the plantation for $190,000 and returned to Tallahassee. After the Civil War, in 1972, Major George Patton acquired the plantation for $3,000 but later abandoned it. It was deeded to the state in 1925 by the United Daughters of the Confederacy.

79

Photo by Kim Cool

G.WIZ is in downtown Sarasota.
  **From Interstate 75 take Exit 210 (Fruitville Road) east
approximately 5 miles to U.S. 41. Turn right and travel north to
Boulevard of the Arts. Turn left (west). G.WIZ will be to the
right, across from the Sarasota Hyatt. There is some parking on
the street as well as in the parking lot next to the building. For
more information, visit www.gwiz.org or call (941) 906-1851.**

G.WIZ

G.WIZ, the Gulfcoast Wonder and Imagination Zone, in Sarasota, will make your hair stand on end.

Possibly haunted by the spirit of Rube Goldberg and other ingenious creators, inventors and scientists, G.WIZ is located immediately south of Sarasota's "purple people seater," the Van Wezel Performing Arts Hall, near the shore of Sarasota Bay. At night its diamond glass windows stand out as much as its Frank Lloyd Wright-designed purple-hued neighbor.

The 33,000-square foot building, the Blivas Science & Technology Center, is a user-friendly space in which visitors of all ages can try their hand at science, sometimes even causing their hair to stand on end.

Goldberg, famous for making contraptions that worked in the most complicated way, would have loved to watch the 15-pound bowling ball that is carried up and down and around a circular area defined by six stations, each connected by a wire mesh tube through which the ball passes en route to the next station. He might have been even more fascinated by the $86,000 cost to create this one attraction — the Machine Village. This Village illustrates several principles of physics.

In other areas of the museum, one can build a robot, erect a giant tower of metal shavings with the help of a strong magnet or fix a toaster.

Or, try your hand(s) at creating your own personal ride. Seated in a chair and holding a spinning wheel, visitors can learn about the power of centrifugal force while becoming a sort of human gyroscope.

Budding aeronautical engineers can launch custom-made paper airplanes and watch them fly — or flop through a pneumatic tube. Learn Clamation cartooning, take apart electric fans, watch experiments. G.WIZ it's fun!

Photo by Kim Cool

A volunteer working as a conductor watches the train pull in to the station at Parish.

From Interstate 75 South, take Exit 229 at Parrish. Travel east on Moccasin Wallow Road to US. 301. From I-75 North, take Exit 224 and travel 7 miles north on US 301. Turn right and then take the next left turn onto 83rd Street. The museum grounds are behind the post office. For more information, visit www.from.org or call (877) 869-0800.

Florida Gulf Coast Railroad Museum

In Parish, grown-ups play with full-sized trains, not models.

Each weekend visitors and volunteers gather at the Florida Gulf Coast Railroad Museum to experience first hand what it was like to ride the rails in Florida half a century or more ago.

The museum on wheels is composed of carefully restored vintage rolling stock and diesel engines that propel the train cars from the Parrish station to Willow, a virtual ghost town that is even smaller than Parrish.

Restored rolling stock includes a 1940s era Pullman sleeper car named the Bradenton, a car that was saved from the scrap heap with just hours to go. The cost was $7,500, far less than what it will cost in money and in-kind labor to restore it to its original appearance.

When it was new, the Bradenton made regular round trips between New York City and Venice on the Silver Meteor route, which was canceled in 1970. In those days the car had deluxe bedrooms with private bathrooms and roomette compartments for single passengers. Its sister car, the Sarasota, was scrapped.

Other FGCRM cars represent the many eras during which there have been trains in Florida.

The museum's mission to acquire, preserve and operate interesting and historic examples of railroad rolling stock, with particular emphasis on the railroads that have served the state of Florida since the 19th century when Henry Flagler brought trains to the east coast and Henry Plant brought railroads to Florida's west coast.

Reservations are generally not necessary for the weekend rides, which depart at 11 a.m. and 2 p.m. each Saturday and Sunday for the 90-minute roundtrip ride.

Train buffs outnumber everyone else and are a source of fascinating stories about the glory days of the iron horses.

Photo by Kim Cool

Mary's Chapel is next to a tiny cemetery in which several early settlers and their families are buried. Ticket sales and a gift shop are located in the former Laurel School near the entrance.

From Interstate 75, take Exit 200 (Laurel Road. Travel west to U.S 41. Turn right. Historic Spanish Point will be on the left at 337 North Tamiami Trail. For more information, including hours and prices, visit www.historicspanishpoint.org or call (941) 966-5214.

Historic Spanish Point

Slather on the sun protection, bring a bottle of water and prepare to go back in time — three times in just one place.

At Historic Spanish Point in Osprey, you will learn what the west coast of Florida was like in prehistoric times, pioneer days and in the 20th century when it was the winter home of Chicago millionaire Bertha Honore Palmer.

Bones and other remnants of prehistoric times plus shell middens showcase the earliest inhabitants of the area, the Calusa Indians. The last of the Calusas died or departed in the late 1800s, as the pioneers arrived from the north to stake their claim as homesteaders in one of the most unwelcoming parts of the United States. Even then, their commercial success was similar to that of today, citrus and tourism. Their names can be found on the gravestones in the tiny cemetery next to Mary's Chapel — Knights, Higels and Webbs.

When Palmer arrived in 1910 as the wealthy widow of hotel magnate and real estate investor Potter Palmer, the futures of Venice and Sarasota were forged. Except for a few hiccups circa 1929-1930 when Florida's land boom met the Great Depression, this area's legacy was sealed. Even though she died in 1918, she was responsible for moving Venice south, naming Nokomis and extending the railroad. That move alone paved the way for the Brotherhood of Locomotive Engineers to discover and develop early Venice.

Palmer's magnificent house is gone but there is still plenty to see, including her rose garden and pergola, the old packing house, chapel, fully restored White cottage, Webb and Guptil houses and a cutaway midden. Most days you also might see boats being built by students and volunteers working in the boat shed along the bay.

Walk or take a tram tour but allow at least a half day there.

Photo by Kim Cool, permission granted by the museum.
The courtyard of The John and Mable Ringling Museum of Art, State Art Museum of Florida.

Take Interstate 75 to Exit 213 (University Parkway). Travel west to the end of the parkway at Bay Shore Road. Parking is available at the adjacent Florida State University Performing Arts Center. For more information, visit www.ringling.org or call (941) 359-5700.

John & Mable Ringling Museum of Art

When real estate and circus mogul John Ringling and his wife, Mable, founded The John and Mable Ringling Museum of Art, they put in motion the first steps to making Sarasota the heart of Florida's culture coast. Today that museum complex is affiliated with Florida State University and is the largest museum/university complex in the United States.

In addition to an art collection ranked in the top 20 in the nation, the complex includes *Ca d'Zan*, the Ringling winter home, a research library, museum stores and the Circus Museums, with the new Tibbals Learning Center. The complex is at the west end of University Parkway.

The museum includes 21 galleries of European and American masterpieces by such artists as Rubens and Van-Dyck. The giant Rubens tapestry cartoons are worth the trip. They fill the walls of galleries 1 and 2 and are magnificent.

Not to be missed is the museum's cloistered central courtyard with its collection of bronze replicas of ancient Greek, Roman and Baroque sculpture from the Chiurazzi Foundry in Naples, Italy. The David replica of the marble original stands guard over the courtyard. Even the doorways leading to the courtyard are works of art and each one is different, just as the museum's interior doorways differ in style and set the stage for each of the various galleries. Solomonic columns flank the entry to the Rubens galleries, considered the grandest of the interior spaces.

After touring the art gallery and *Ca d'Zan* mansion, enjoy lunch. Then spend time in the Circus Museums, learning about the man who made Sarasota the circus capital of the world. Circus families still impact the region. The Tibbals collection and the reinstallation of the 18th century Asolo Theatre complete the not-to-be-missed complex. The museum is open daily except Thanksgiving, Christmas and New Year's Day.

Photo by Kim Cool

The Payne Mansion at Marie Selby Botanical Gardens
was recently restored.

From Interstate 75, take Exit 210 (SR 780, Fruitville).
Travel West to U.S. 41 (Tamiami Trail). Turn right and travel
north to Palm Avenue. Turn left. There are several parking areas
at left. The gardens are on your right at 811 S. Palm Ave. For
more information, visit www.selby.org or call 366-5731.

Marie Selby Botanical Gardens

Marie Selby Botanical Gardens is world-renowned as an epiphyte and bromeliad center.

Located on the edge of Sarasota Bay in downtown Sarasota, the gardens, working greenhouses, plant shop and indoor display gardens fill the 8.5-acre peninsula. It was once the site of the homes of Marie and Bill Selby and Christy and Ann Payne. The former Payne house has been restored and is used for special events throughout the year.

The outdoor gardens include many palm trees, stands of giant bamboo that make magical music when the wind blows, a fernery, butterfly gardens, herb garden, hibiscus garden and a medicinal plant garden. There are many edible plants and a treehouse that is wheelchair accessible.

Garden benches throughout the grounds invite visitors to sit awhile to fully take in the serene setting and escape their cares, if only for a few minutes.

This is the place to learn about tropical gardening. There are plenty of experts on hand to assist visitors and answer questions. They help with plant identification, hold classes on tropical plants, nature printing, bonsai and other related subjects throughout the year. Three annual plant sales allow visitors the opportunity to grow plants they have seen at Selby in their own gardens or homes.

Selby truly is everything its visitors need it to be — refuge, learning center, garden center, plant doctor and source of rare plants and information. No wonder it is world famous.

An indoor garden area replicates conditions found in the rain forest and is filled with still more tropical plants.

Be sure to visit the book shop and snack bar before or after signing up for classes or field trips.

Selby's mission is to make a difference. It does it well.

Photo by Kim Cool

From Interstate 75, take Exit 210 (SR 780, Fruitville). Travel West to U.S. 41 (Tamiami Trail) and along Sarasota Bay to the John Ringling Causeway. Take the Ringling Causeway over the bridge to St. Armands Circle. Watch for signs to Mote and to Longboat Key, the first right off the circle (John Ringling Boulevard). Ken Thompson Parkway will be at the next traffic light. Turn right. Mote's main entrance will be on your right. For more information, visit www.mote.org or call 388-2451.

Mote Marine Laboratory

They study marine life — and death — at Mote Marine Laboratory. Both a public attraction and a scientific research facility, Mote has come along way from its humble beginnings in Placida nearly a half century ago.

Headquartered in Sarasota, Mote also has a center in Key West and, with the help of trained volunteers, covers the waterfront of much of Florida.

Its trained turtle patrollers make a serious difference in the protection of endangered sea turtles nesting and hatching along Florida beaches from May 1 to Oct. 31

Its resident scientists study everything from sea turtles to red tide and anything else that affects marine life.

Visitors can watch the scientists at work and also see rescued manatees and turtles.

As an attraction, Mote allows visitors to see manatees and turtles in rehabilitation tanks but also offers visitors the chance to get up close to several aquariums designed to showcase artificial reefs, grassflats, dynamic coastlines, rivers, bays and estuaries and the creatures that inhabit those special places. More than 260,000 visitors come to Mote annually.

Good signage and well-lit tanks allow those visitors to see even the shyest creatures and to learn more about them. Guides are plentiful and knowledgeable, ready and willing to answer myriads of questions about the aquariums and their inhabitants. More than 1,000 volunteers serve Mote as guides, regularly taking continuing education courses to improve their knowledge.

View sharks from above and from the side. Touch a stingray (the barbs have been removed) and pick up a starfish in a special touch tank. Children love the Touch Tank housing little sea creatures, some in their shells.

Plan at least a half-day visit to Mote.

Photo by Kim Cool

The Pelican Man's Bird Sanctuary shares its main driveway with Mote Marine Laboratory.

From Interstate 75, take Exit 210 (SR 780, Fruitville). Travel West to U.S. 41 (Tamiami Trail) and along Sarasota Bay to the John Ringling Causeway. Take the Ringling Causeway over the bridge to St. Armands Circle. Watch for signs to Mote, the first right off the circle (John Ringling Boulevard). Ken Thompson Parkway will be at the next traffic light. Turn right. Pelican Man's Bird Sanctuary will be on your right, next to Mote. For more information, visit www.pelicanman.org or call (941) 388-4444.

Pelican Man's Bird Sanctuary

The largest wildlife rescue and rehabilitation center in Florida happened because one man, Dale Shields, was for the birds, and the wildlife.

Shields, who passed away in 2003, literally could talk to the animals and they could talk to him. It began in 1981 when he was fishing and found an injured pelican. Finding no organization to help the bird, he nursed it back to health in his own bathtub. He released it back into the wild some weeks later. It was the first of thousands of birds he would save. But first he had his own brush with death, during which he pledged to devote his life to helping sick and injured wildlife if he would live. He did live and the sanctuary grew from his promise.

That first pelican seems to have spread the word, for some 200 sick and injured pelicans found their way to Shields' apartment soon after he rescued that first one — dubbed "George."

When his yard became overcrowded, the town of Longboat Key donated some property for the first sanctuary. When that too became overcrowded, the City of Sarasota leased Shields three acres of land on City Island for $1 a year for a permanent sanctuary. It has been there ever since 1989, just across the parking lot from Mote Marine Laboratory.

Sanctuary employees and volunteers respond to 9,000 calls per year. Two trucks are on the road daily from St. Petersburg to Englewood and North Port. Approximately 5,000 birds are rescued and helped each year. Nearly all are released back to the wild. Those that cannot be released are cared for at the sanctuary as long as they live. Those birds and other creatures make up most of the display for visitors. Birds to be released are kept away from people.

Honored by President George Bush in 1990, Shields was awarded the 184th Point of Light Award.

Photo by Kim Cool

Designed by Frank Lloyd Wright's Taliesan team of designers, the seashell-shaped auditorium known as the Van Wezel Performing Arts Hall is the best-know landmark along Sarasota Bay in the heart of Florida's Cultural Coast. The color was chosen by Wright's wife from the inside of a seashell she found in the area.

Performing Arts Venues

Asolo Theatre Company, Cook and Mertz Theatres, 5555 North Tamiami Trail, Sarasota, www.asolo.org, (941) 351-8000

Banyan Theater Company, (summer theater) Sarasota, www.banyantheatercompany, (941) 358-5330

Circus Sarasota, www.circussarasota.org, (941) 355-9335.

Florida Studio Theatre, 1241 N. Palm Ave., Sarasota, www.fst2000.org, (941) 366-9000

Florida West Coast Symphony, 709 North Tamiami Trail, Sarasota, www.fwcs.org, (941) 953-4252

Golden Apple Dinner Theatre, 25 N. Pineapple Ave., Sarasota, www.thegodenapple.com, (941) 366-5454

La Musica International Chamber Music, Sarasota, www.lamusicafestival.org, (941) 366-8450, Ext. 3

Lemon Bay Playhouse, 96 W. Dearborn St., Englewood, www.lemonbayplayhouse.com, (941) 475-6756

Manatee Players, 102 Old Main St., Bradenton, www.manateeplayers.com, (941) 748-0111

Sarasota Ballet of Florida, 5555 North Tamiami Trail, Sarasota www.sarasotaballet.org, (941) 359-0099

Sarasota Film Society, 506 Burns Lane, www.filmsociety.org, (941) 955-3456

Sarasota Opera, Sarasota Opera House, 61 Pineapple Ave., www.sarasotaopera.org, (941) 366-8450

The Players Theatre, 838 North Tamiami Trail, Sarasota, www.theplayers.org, (941) 365-2494

Van Wezel Performing Arts Hall, 777 North Tamiami Trail, Sarasota, www.vanwezel.org, (941) 953-3368

Venice Little Theatre, 140 W. Tampa Ave., www.venicestage.com, (941) 488-1115

Photo By Kim Cool

Sarasota's **Ed Smith Stadium** is the spring training home of the Cincinnati Reds and the summer home of the Sarasota Red Sox.

From Interstate 75, take Exit 210 (Fruitville). Travel west to Tuttle Road. Turn right and travel north to 12th Street, The stadium complex will be to your left. The parking entrance is from Tuttle but you have to make a U-turn to get there on the divided road.

Professional Sports

Auto Racing

DeSoto Super Speedway Inc., 21000 East State Road 64, Bradenton, (941) 748-3171.

Dog Racing

Sarasota Kennel Club, 5400 Old Bradenton Road, (941) 355-7744.

Baseball - Spring Training

Cincinnati Reds, Ed Smith Stadium, 2700 12th Street, Sarasota http://cincinnati.reds.mlb.com, (941) 954-4464.

Pittsburgh Pirates, McKechnie Field, 1611 Ninth St. West, Bradenton, http://pittsburgh.pirates.mlb.com, (941) 748-4610.

Minor League Baseball - Florida State League

Sarasota Red Sox, Ed Smith Stadium, 2700 12th Street, Sarasota www.sarasox.com, (941) 954-4460.

Water skiing shows

Sarasota Ski-A-Rees, Ken Thompson Park behind Mote Marine Laboratory, www.skiarees.com, (941) 388-1666.

Photo by Kim Cool

John and Mable Ringling drove this Rolls Royce Silver Ghost from 1921-1926. It had a 150.5-inch wheelbase. It can be seen at the Sarasota Car Museum.

From Interstate 75, take Exit 213 (University Parkway). Travel west 7 miles to U.S. 41. The museum is on the right at 5500 North Tamiami Trail. For more information, visit sarasotacarmuseum.org or call (941) 355-6228.

Sarasota Car Museum

Your first car could be at the Sarasota Car Museum, even if you have yet to acquire that first car.

Having turned the half-century mark, the museum has some of the oldest cars made. But, some of more recent vintage cars will inspire memories in anyone who has driven a car for awhile, and other cars will whet the appetite of youngsters approaching their driving years. Restored to the way they were when new, these are cars to dream about and drool over.

Located on North Tamiami Trail across from the John and Mable Ringling Museum of Art and the Florida State University Center for the Performing Arts, the 60,000-square-foot building sits on 4 acres of land and is as different as night and day.

By day it is a classic car museum in which visitors can get up close to prototype cars, famous race cars, classic old-time Model Ts and cars of the rich and famous. Of special interest to those familiar with the Ringling name are several cars that once belonged to John and Mable, including her 1923 Pierce Arrow and their 1921 Rolls Royce Silver Ghost. One Ringling Rolls awaits restoration.

By night, the museum becomes a banquet and event facility in which guests can dance among the Dodges and Dusenbergs.

Among the treasures is a Mercedes Roadster that once belonged to Beatle John Lennon and a smaller Morris belonging to fellow Beatle Paul McCartney.

Each car is identified with a sign attesting to its age, make, model, ownership and additional pertinent facts.

Should you like a car so much you want to take it home, you might be able to, for a short time and for a price. Several museum cars are available for limousine service to those who would like to make a really grand entrance.

A huge gift shop filled with an eclectic assortment of car-themed and other collectibles completes the package.

Photo by Kim Cool

Flora, fauna and flamingos inside the Sarasota city limits. From Interstate 75, take Fruitville Road to U.S. 41 in downtown Sarasota. Turn right and travel north to Myrtle Street. Turn left and follow the signs .25 mile to the entrance, which will be on the left. For more information, visit www.sarsotajunglegardens.com or call (941) 355-5305.

Sarasota Jungle Gardens

The only zoological garden in the area also can claim the title of the oldest attraction in Sarasota.

It looks, smells and sounds like a real jungle yet covers just 10 acres within the city limits. Native animals like squirrels scamper freely through the gardens, while less friendly creatures such as leopards and alligators and crocodiles are confined — to be seen but not touched.

During one of the twice-daily Reptile Encounter shows some lucky visitor might even go home with a piece of snake skin. Others might get to hold a very young alligator. During one show, we learned that there are 1.3 million alligators in Florida but no native crocodiles. There is one crocodile so visitors can compare it to Florida's native alligators.

The Reptile Encounter is one of five shows that are performed twice daily in special grandstand areas located throughout the gardens.

Other shows include Birds of Prey, Critters & Things and Birds of the Rainforest. Once injured, sick and unable to care for themselves, the gardens' birds of prey were given to the gardens as their last refuge. There, they receive the expert care they need to survive.

Twice daily, the keepers come out to meet the public at various points within the gardens.

At other times, visitors can simply enjoy the winding walkways through the jungle or sit awhile to savor the scents and sounds of this unique place.

Plan to spend a full day if you intend to view all the shows, have a snack, feed the koi and give the children time to enjoy the playground, have a pony ride or to pose with a parrot. Even a quick run-through of the gardens will take at least two hours. A shell collection is displayed in the building housing the snack bar.

Sarasota Jungle Gardens, 3701 Bay Shore Road, Sarasota, is open every day but Christmas, from 9 a.m.-5 p.m.

Photo by Kim Cool

Every Thursday, banjo players lure hundreds of fans to Snook Haven for music and lunch.

Take Interstate 75 to Exit 191 (River Road). Travel West to Venice Avenue. The entrance to Snook Haven will be on your left. During the season, you might need to park there and be shuttled to the restaurant. For more information, call 485-7221.

Snook Haven

Prepare to be strung along — especially on Thursday. That is the day that banjo players nearly outnumber the folks who come to watch them. At the height of the winter season, as many as 70 or 80 banjo players may be there, strumming away while their ardent fans sing along.

Snook Haven is a fish camp like no other. Little more than a decade ago, that is all it was. Not anymore.

Since owner Sandy Cotton took over the old restaurant, bar, boat livery and fish camp, things have changed.

On a typical day there are as many senior citizens as bikers, as many Mercedes as Harleys, as many pick-up trucks as fancy SUVs.

And on Thursday, the banjo players are there at lunchtime. Finding a place to park becomes a challenge well before noon. At times like that a shuttle bus goes into service, bringing folks from the parking lot out on River Road back to the restaurant on the Myakka River. If the weather is good, and it nearly always is, everyone sits outside on large picnic tables, eating hamburgers and quarter-pound hot dogs, fried shrimp or gator bites washed down with beer or iced tea. Sandy and her husband Don have counted as many as 650 for the weekly "practice" sessions. The Cottons provide lunch for the players during their 12:15-12:45 pm. break.

The oldest player is 90-year-old Ollie Austin who also performs at Snook Haven on Saturday evenings, with Sandy on the piano and Bud Nelson on guitar.

Everyday is different at Snook Haven — customer-wise and entertainment-wise.

The details are on the menus, which list the food and drinks, entertainment schedule, boat rental and charter prices and Myakka Queen tour rates.

Photo by Kim Cool

Meet King Solomon in his castle.
Take Interstate 75 to Exit 220a (Wauchuka/Zolfo
Springs). Had east on SR 64 to CR 665. Travel South to SR 655,
make a hard left and travel North 100 feet. Bear right on
Solomon Road. Go Northeast for .4 miles. For more information,
visit solomonscastle.com or call (863) 494-6077.

Solomon's Castle

All the news that was fit to print in a local newspaper now covers the walls of Ona, Florida's architectural wonder, Solomon's Castle.

Built entirely by hand by famed sculptor Howard Solomon, the shiny printing-plate-covered castle has a tower, stained glass windows and a moat. When not using old printing plates for his work, Solomon might use old oil drums or other findings as he turns trash to treasure in his studio. Also in the castle are the family living quarters and several galleries filled with Solomon's collection of found objects.

The castle grounds were designed by Peggy Solomon and include a nature trail along picturesque Horse Creek. There is a drawbridge over the moat, connecting the castle to the nature trail. Sculptures and whimsical creatures nestle within the garden beds and beneath the Spanish moss hanging from the gardens' live oak trees. There is even a boat in the moat.

And, better yet, given the off-the-beaten-path location of the castle, that boat is the Solomons' Boat in the Moat restaurant, which is open from 11 a.m.-4 p.m. on the days the castle is open. The restaurant is within the boat, a replica of a 60-foot 16th century Spanish Galleon. It, too, features stained glass windows. Solomon's daughter Alane is the cook.

For those who can't bear to leave the castle, the Solomons offer lodging on the top floor in the Blue Moon Room. It has a private balcony overlooking the moat, paintings of unicorns and knights in shining armor on the closet doors and even a view of the space shuttle if the day is clear and there is a shuttle launch.

Souvenirs can be purchased in the castle's gift shop.

Photo by Kim Cool

The Triangle Inn, home of the Venice Archives and Area Historical Collection is at 351 S. Nassau St.

From Interstate 75, take Exit 193 (Jacaranda Boulevard.) Travel south on Jacaranda to East Venice Avenue. Turn right and head west over the bridge onto the island of Venice. Turn left on Nassau Street and head south to the Triangle Inn. For more information, visit www.veniceflorida.com/community/archive.htm or call (941) 486-2487.

Venice Archives

Saved from the wrecking ball, the former Triangle Inn was moved to its present site in 1991. After five years of restoration and renovation, the circa 1927 rooming house or bed and breakfast was converted to house the city's archives and collection of historic artifacts.

The mission of the Venice Archives and Area historical Collection is to collect and preserve historical and archeological material relating to Venice and the communities of Nokomis, Laurel and Osprey, whose histories have been interwoven from 1867 to the present.

Manuscript collections comprise the bulk of the historical collection and have been cataloged by volunteers under the direction of the city's archivist. Dorothy Korwek currently holds that position. Also included in the collection are papers, records, letters, photo albums and other artifacts donated to the archives by residents and family members of residents or former residents. In recent years, a collection of oral histories was begun and VCR tapes were made of local events.

A vertical file of carefully indexed newspaper clippings augments the archive's collection of the Venice News (1926-1928 and the Venice Gondolier (1946-1986).

The Triangle Inn's Mediterranean Revival Style architecture is representative of the buildings constructed in the mid 1920s when Venice was being promoted and developed by the Brotherhood of Locomotive Engineers. It is stucco over frame with a concrete barrel tile roof and double hung windows.

Open two or three days each week, depending on the season, the building offers historic displays, occasional historic tours and research help for those interested in learning more about the history of the greater Venice area and its people.

The building is owned by the city of Venice.

Kim Cool

Part IV
Discover the
Platinum Coast

Photo By Kim Cool

Fans propel the airboats over the top of the water.
From Interstate 75, take Exit 80 (SR 29). Head south on
SR 29 toward Everglades City. Capt. Doug's Everglades Tours
will be on the left, 1 mile past the Bridge on SR 29. For more
information, visit www.captaindougs.com or call (800) 282-9194.

Airboat Rides

Airboat tours in the Everglades City area are as easy to find as alligators - but much more fun.

The oldest company offering such narrated scenic tours of the Everglades River area is Captain Doug's Small Airboat & Scenic Boat Tours.

Captain Doug House is from an old Everglades family. His ancestors arrived in the area in 1850, farming on one of the Ten Thousand Islands, now known as House's Hammock.

The House family has been an integral part of Everglades City, House's Hammock and the neighboring island, Chokolo-skee, for more than a century,

Captain Doug also is a long-time professional fishing guide in the Everglades as well as the founder of the airboat tour company, the first such company in the area.

With a U.S. Coast Guard licensed captain and experienced guide, you will tour along the mangrove-edged waters of the Everglades River, photographing native plants such as the mangroves and see many of the creatures that inhabit the waters, including alligators and swimming and wading birds.

The price of the airboat tour includes a visit to Captain Doug's Alligator Park and Indian Village. In the alligator show, spectators can see the ancient creatures up close and learn more about them and their habits and habitats.

Be sure to wear plenty of sunscreen and if you wear a hat, make sure it is one that will not blow off when you are literally flying over the water on the airboat. The boats lift above the sawgrass and into the air, moving at high speed.

Airboats are loud, so consider bringing earplugs.

Unless you are staying in Everglades City, plan a day trip. It takes a while to get there and you will want to make the most of it.

Photo by Kim Cool

Take I-75 to Exit 164. Travel East on U.S. 17 to S.R.74, which goes off to the right as U.S. 17 heads North. Your time on S.R. 74 will seem like the longest part of the trip as it is a two-lane road with a 55 mph speed limit. At Babcock Corner, turn right onto S.R. 31. The ranch will be on your left. Continue 6 miles to the entrance to Babcock Wilderness Adventures. For more information, visit www.babcockwilderness.com or call (800) 500-5583.

Babcock Wilderness Adventures

At Babcock Wilderness Adventures, on a 90,000-acre working ranch that straddles Lee and Charlotte counties, visitors come face-to-face with panthers, Florida cracker cattle, birds and wild alligators — mostly from the safety of old school buses, rebuilt as "swamp buggies."

The ranch is the Crescent B. It produces lumber, vegetables, sod, calves in addition to entertaining tourists on its swamp buggy rides.

The ranch is so big that its cowboys are trucked to the areas they must patrol by horseback each day. The swamp buggy rides cover only a small fraction of the 12- by 14-mile property.

Within the tourist area visited by the swamp buggies is an alligator-filled swamp and a group of old-style buildings housing a swamp museum, reptile exhibit, old ranch implements, a gift shop and the Gator Shack restaurant. The restaurant serves up breaded and deepfried fresh alligator bites at lunchtime. For the squeamish, the restaurant also serves burgers and fries.

The building housing the museum was in the movie "Just Cause" starring Sean Connery. Non-native orchids planted by the film crew remain in the swamp as proof that the Hollywood types were there.

More intriguing to most visitors is Lulu, the three-horned cow that died Sept. 30, 1991, at the ripe old age of 24. In her youth, a third horn grew from the middle of her forehead. It is said that she "kept it polished on the posterior of any Levi's within reach." She never bore any three-horned heirs, despite the breeding attempts of the ranch's owner.

Tours operate daily from November-May, from 9 a.m.-3 p.m. Reservations are a must.

Most of the tour is by swamp buggy except for a brief stop to wander back to the panther cages via a boardwalk above the swamp.

P:hoto courtesy of Clyde Butcher Gallery

From Interstate 75, take Exit 101 (SR 951) toward Marco Island. At U.S> 41 (Tamiami Trail), head east (there will be a Publix and a KMart Plaza). Get gas first as the gallery is 47 miles east, juast past the Big Cypress Preserve Oasis Visitors Center on the north (left) side of the road. The gallery is on the right at 52388 Tamiami Trail. For more information, visit www.clydebutcher.com or call (239) 695-2428 or (888)999-9113. Fir the Venice Gallery, call (941) 486-0811.

Big Cypress Gallery

Florida's foremost wildlife photographer Clyde Butcher shoots big and prints the results even bigger. He uses a large-format camera to capture the stunning black and white nature studies that have solidified his reputation as one of the country's premier photographers. Once captured on 8- by 10-inc, 11- by 14-inch or 12- by 20-inch photographic plates, he uses custom-made enlargers to make those images even larger, resulting in silver gelatin photographic prints ranging in size from 48 by 48 inches to 5 by 9 feet,

With galleries in Venice and in the Big Cypress Swamp, Butcher, with his wife Nicki, has developed a relationship with nature that restored his soul after his son Ted was killed by a drunk driver in 1986. He would escape into the swamp for days at a time. Butcher's spiritual experiences during that time reinforced his dedication to use his photographs to inspire others to preserve such special places as the Florida Everglades for future generations.

Each fall, he leads groups of photographers and nature lovers into the swamp to share what he found there, "the swamp's soul." Space on these rare day trips is often filled months in advance by people of all walks of life. Most are entering the swamp for the first time. Many will return.

The architecture graduate of California Polytechnic University in San Luis Obisbo today lives on the edge of the Big Cypress Swamp.

He maintains a dark room and gallery there as well as in Venice. Butcher's work has been shown at museums across the country and featured in many books and publications. Limited edition prints of his work are printed on fiber base paper and selenium toned for archival preservation.

Butcher is an artist, an environmentalist and so much more.

Photo by Kim Cool

The former Charlotte Harbor & Northern Railway Depot.
From Interstate 75, take Exit 179 (Toledo Blade
Boulevard). Travel south to U.S. 41 and turn left, continuing
south to S.R. 776 at Murdock. Turn right and follow that until it
makes a sharp right at the junction with S.R. 771. Follow 771
toward Placida and watch for signs to the bridge to Boca
Grande. The causeway leads into Gasparilla Road. At Fifth
Street, turn left and then right at East Railroad Avenue.

Boca Grande Railroad Depot

While enjoying lunch outside at the Loose Caboose, diners can see the last piece of railroad track in what was once a "Railroad Town" and destination for the old Charlotte Harbor and Northern Railway. It is another of Florida's "Ghost railroads," so-called because they are gone. The former depot remains — on East Railroad Avenue at the corner of Fourth Street.

You can walk on these tracks without fear of a train coming along for the track to and from nowhere is just a block long. But it is there and so is the old circa 1913 depot, restored for its new life as a retail hub in the heart of town.

In addition to the Loose Caboose restaurant and its companion ice cream shop, the building contains several boutiques and at least one of the many real estate offices. They are plentiful in this pricey island community. Boca Grande hosts many of the rich and famous, including the George Bush family. Both presidents have been spending winter breaks here for years.

You will pay a price to go there. A toll bridge at the entrance to Gasparilla Island greets you before the rather long drive into town. Maybe it is the toll bridge itself, or the fact that it seems as though it takes forever to get there, but Boca Grande feels different than most other gulf coast communities.

Once there, plan to spend some time, even if the only thing you do is drive up and down a few of the streets and look at the homes and churches. Better yet, park the car and walk a bit, enjoying lunch outside at the "Loose" or one of several other places offering *al fresco* dining.

At the southern tip of the island is the Boca Grande Light House and Museum at Gasparilla State Recreation Area. The water you see is Charlotte Harbor and just off shore is where the famous Boca Grande tarpon tournaments are held. Boca Grande bills itself as the "Tarpon Fishing Capital of the World."

Photo courtesy of Caribbean Gardens

Ruffled Lemurs and other primates dwell at the Naples zoo. From Interstate 75, take Exit 107 (CR 896 Pine Ridge Road). Go west just under 4 miles to Goodlette-Frank Road. Turn left, heading south. The zoo is on the left about 3 miles ahead, one block south of the Golden Gate Parkway at 1590 Goodlette-Frank Road. For more information, visit www.caribbeangardens.com or call (239) 262-5409.

Caribbean Gardens (Naples Zoo)

Clevelanders who remember "Jungle" Larry Tetzloff and his wife "Safari" Jane will be right at home at Caribbean Gardens in Naples. When the Tetzloffs left Cleveland, Ohio for warmer climes, they headed to Naples. There they introduced rare animals to the botanical gardens that were started in 1919 by Dr. Henry Nehrling.

The result was a true zoological garden filled with extraordinary flora and fauna. Nationally accredited, it contains a 52-acre jungle of exotic plants, many dating to 1918 when Nehrling started his garden. When Jungle Larry arrived, the setting was perfect for showcasing lions and kangaroos and monkeys and exotics like Asian deer that bark and eat meat.

Whether you book a private animal encounter in advance of your visit or simply go to any of the daily programs, you will come away with new-found knowledge about both plants and animals. Master gardeners and zoo keepers regularly share their expertise just as Jungle Larry used to do on Cleveland TV and later at the Naples Zoo. These keepers encourage you to arrive with questions.

Be sure to catch a ride on one of the catamarans that cruise through the islands of primates living in natural habitats. The cruise is included with the price of admission so you can take it several times if you wish. If it is a hot day, you may want to spend a lot of time on the catamaran, but in the heat of the day, you many not see much as the primates will be napping. Heat affects the animals too. They will be more active on cooler days so if you want to catch them at their perkiest, visit on a cool day or come early in the morning.

Bring sunscreen, sunglasses and a hat as you will be outdoors. Feed yourself in the zoo's own Subway, but do not feed the animals.

Photo by Kim Cool

If left untouched the Banyan tree given to Thomas Edison by Harvey Firestone in 1925 would cover the estate. It is the largest in the United States.

From Interstate 75 take Exit 136 (SR 884, Colonial Boulevard). Travel West to McGregor Boulevard. Turn right and travel approximately 2 miles. The estates will be on the right. For more information, visit www.edison-ford-estate.com or call (239) 334-3614.

Edison & Ford Winter Estates

Neighbors and friends Thomas Alva Edison and Henry Ford left the city of Fort Myers a valuable tourist attraction and a nickname — the City of Palms.

The Edison & Ford Winter Estates, newly restored, is the city's chief tourist attraction.

Located along the shore of the Caloosahatchee River, the 14-acre property straddles both sides of MacGregor Boulevard. The palm-lined street became responsible for the nickname after Edison purchased 1,800 Royal Palms from Cuba and gave them to the city to line both sides of the street.

Listed on the National Register of Historic Homes, the estates also have been designated a Florida Heritage Landmark.

The site is the eighth most-visited historic home in the United States, drawing more than 250,000 visitors each year.

In addition to the two mirror image houses where the Edisons and Fords wintered for two weeks per year, the historic site also has a carriage house with several old Ford automobiles. An older home, original to the property, plus a long pier out into the Caloosahatchee River are other interests. Make a day of it and take the two-hour electric launch on the river.

The welcome center is across the street. Also there is Edison's laboratory, the office where he spent most of his waking hours and a museum. Edison earned at least one patent per year for some 65 years. Examples of his inventions are in the museum and in the laboratory.

Guides and actors add to the experience. You might see Mrs. Ford herself in the Ford living room. The guided tours last about 90 minutes and include the buildings and the grounds, which contain myriad plants including a sausage tree from Africa, frangi-pangi, chenille bush, cannonball tree, mango tree, vanilla beans and bamboo for lightbulb filiaments.

121

Photo by Kim Cool

Susie's Station Restaurant, located directly across from City Hall in the heart of town, is the place to go to experience old Florida in food and atmosphere.

Take Interstate 75 to Exit 80 (Highway 29). Follow that road right into the city. Susie's will be on the left.

Everglades City

Take the road less traveled. When you get to the end of it, you will be very close to Everglades City, a place where time stands still.

At one end of the Wilderness Waterway, which links the city to Flamingo, Everglades City bills itself as the "Gateway to the 10,000 Islands". It may well be the best place from which to check out those islands, whether by floatplane, kayak, canoe or airboat.

Following the arrival of Barron Collier in 1923, the city prospered as a mecca for tourists and sportsmen even as Collier transformed the town with the addition of a railroad, bank, telephone, sawmills, churches, boatyard, school and more.

More recently, the establishment of Everglades National Park and the purchase of the Big Cypress Swamp and 10,000 Islands for conservation set in motion another growth spurt. Everglades City is an ecotourism center in SW Florida.

Lodging varies from motels to B&Bs and a day spa offers a place to soothe muscles unaccustomed to canoeing and kayaking. History buffs will enjoy the Museum of the Everglades, located since 1998 in the Old Laundry, a building that is older than the Tamiami Trail. The museum is open Tuesday-Saturday.

Fishing may be as big a pastime as paddling, but bigger yet is seafood consumption. The city is known as the Stone Crab Capital of Florida and celebrates that fact with an annual stone crab festival.

For good food and great atmosphere, have a grouper sandwich at Susie's Station Restaurant, right across the street from City Hall. Sit in a booth surrounded by old gasoline pumps and other memorabilia from the early days of this old city. For dessert — key lime pie of course.

Photo by Dennis Gardner

This depot in Fort Myers was saved to live a new life as a museum.

From interstate 75, take Exit 141 (Palm Beach Boulevard) west toward 5 miles toward Ft. Myers/Harborside. Turn left on Fowler Street and then right on to Dr. Martin Luther King Jr. Boulevard (SR 82 West). Turn left onto Jackson Street for one tenth mile and then right on to Peck Street. If driving from the Fort Myers Historical Museum, take U.S. 41 (Cleveland Avenue) south to Gladiolus. Turn right. The park is at 7330 Gladiolus Drive, on the right. For more park information, visit www.captiva.com/stateparks/lakespark.htm or call (941) 432-2000.

Fort Myers Railroad attractions

In addition to the Seminole Gulf Railroad excursion and mystery trains, which warrant their own article, Fort Myers has two other places of interest to road trippers of the rail variety.

Fort Myers Historical Museum is located downtown in the old railroad station at Jackson and Peck. It is a general interest museum, but the fact that the station has survived when so many Florida stations have been torn down is reason enough to visit.

For more information about the museum, visit www.city-fortmyers.com/attractions/historical, or call (239) 332-5955. The museum's address is 2300 Peck St.

At Lakes County Park on Cypress Lake Drive west of U.S. 41, the Lakes Park Museum Project has recently added a Train Village, with an operating 7.5-inch gauge miniature railroad and a former ACL switcher No. 143 on display.

The miniature train takes passengers on a 15-minute ride over a 1.5-mile track. At one point, the train goes through a 109-foot tunnel. It also goes over several bridges, around a lake, past miniature villages and through the park itself. Wildlife often can be seen from the train.

The miniature railroad is open Tuesday-Friday from 10 a.m.-2 p.m. and until 4 p.m. on Saturday. Sunday it is open from noon-4 p.m.

While visiting the park, be sure to spend some time in the fragrance garden. Created in 1991, wholly with volunteer labor, it was designed as a place where everyone could smell, feel and even eat herbs and flowers.

Also in the park is a boardwalk that offers visitors the opportunity to see fish and wildlife.

Canoeing, picnicking, swimming and fishing are available for visitors to this 158-acre park.

Photo by Dennis Gardner

The entrance to Four Mile Cove Ecological Preserve.
From Interstate 75, take Exit 136 (Colonial Boulevard).
Travel west on Colonial past the toll plaza. Colonial then becomes Veterans Parkway. Take the first right past the toll plaza (SE 17th Place) and then take the first right from there on to SE 23 Terrace. The preserve is at the end of the road. For more information, visit www.capecoral.net/citydept/parks/pks_4mile.cfm or, from October-May, call (239) 549-4606.

Other times, call (239) 549-4606.

Four Mile Cove Ecological Preserve

Watch out for hitch-hiking mullet. Jumping mullet have been known to hop into a passing kayak while the paddler is busy looking at a family of manatees playing in the warm water.

At Four Mile Cove Ecological Preserve in Cape Coral, kayakers and canoers can experience that and more on Saturdays and Sundays when those watercraft are available to rent at the park's kayak shack. The preserve contains 365 acres of unspoiled wetlands and mangrove swamps. Much of it can be seen from the boardwalk but to see it all, you really can't beat a canoe or kayak.

While paddling through a mangrove forest, one might also see a mother alligator and her brood of baby gators just beyond a thicket of mangrove roots, or a harmless water snake sunning itself on a tree branch. An ibis may be roosting nearby. For those who want to get back to nature, it doesn't get any better than this. From a kayak or a canoe you can see things that you could never see any other way, not even from the boardwalk in this park. Classes are offered for beginning kayakers and the last rental departs at 2 p.m.

Open year round from 8 a.m.-sunset, Four Mile Cove offers free admission to its nature trails and boardwalk. A trail guide and displays of local wildlife area available at the visitor center. The boardwalk includes an observation stop at Four Mile Creek. a new pier overlooks the water and three remodeled shelters accessible only by canoe or kayak.

Follow the 4,500-foot walking trail through the mangroves to the original observation pier on the Caloosahatchee River. When you exit the wilderness you will arrive at the Iwo Jima statue and an armed services memorial flag park.

Picnic in the park and then take home some nature related gifts of Florida native plants from the gift shop.

Photo by Kim Cool

When you spot the water tower, you will know you are nearly there.

From Interstate 75, take Exit 138 (Martin Luther King Jr. Boulevard). Travel west for 4 miles to 2000 Cranford Avenue. Turn left. The entrance and parking will be to the right. For more information, visit www.cityftmyers.com/attractions/imaginarium.aspx or call (239) 337-3332.

Imaginarium

Imagine feeling the force of a hurricane, touching a cloud or running through a thunderstorm. You can do all that and more at Fort Myers' hands-on science museum, the Imaginarium.

Allow several hours, especially if you have young children. They will want to do it all, probably twice, and with more than 60 interactive exhibits plus live fish, sharks, turtles, swans, iguanas and more, doing everything once will take long enough.

As an example of something you may want to do more than once. Join your fellow visitors in the hurricane chamber and get a new hairdo in less than 45 seconds, while wearing safety goggles and watching a beachball react to the 45 mph winds generated by a giant fan. The real wind was much worse during any of the four hurricanes that battered Florida in 2004. Since the chamber is not the real thing, most visitors want to do it at least once more before they leave. I did.

If a hurricane is not enough, experience a thunderstorm — indoors, and stay dry during the process.

Or, study the orange trees outside. There really is a little something for everyone at this museum.

Get up close and personal with a moray eel. Check out the coral reef or the koi fish swimming about, accompanied by a turtle, some catfish and two swans — one white and one black. There also is a reptile retreat and an aquarium that invites one to sit awhile to see the nurse shark, slider turtles and two good-sized moray eels. There is a touch tank where you can pick up a horseshoe crab, spotted whelk and other sea creatures.

Most of the museum has been built recently but one interesting section dates to 1938 when the site held the local water treatment plant. The remaining corroded pipes are now part of the new museum and interesting in themselves.

Photo by Kim Cool

Watch for manatees from this open-sided tour boat at Manatee World near Fort Myers.

Take Interstate 75 Exit 141, S.R. 80 (Palm Beach Boulevard). Go east, under the interstate and look for the big orange building on the left. There is a large manatee painted on the front of the building. Before pulling into the parking lot, watch for oncoming traffic which comes over the hill, often at speed. For more information, call (941)694-4042 or visit www.manateeworld.com.

Manatee World

Get up close to one of the most lovable and also rarest animals in Florida at Manatee World near Fort Myers.

Your best opportunity to see these little known and most endangered animals is when the weather is a bit chilly. When the water cools down in the Gulf of Mexico, manatees look for warmer water, heading south and, near Fort Myers, swimming up the Caloosahatchee River toward the Orange River where water is discharged from an electrical power plant. That water is not only warm but also purified. Manatees live in both fresh and salt water but, given the choice, they seem to prefer fresh water — warm fresh water most of all.

Boat tours last about 1.5 hours. Wear a jacket to keep out the wind and sunscreen even though the boat's roof offers some protection. You will be touring with experts who have worked to save the endangered mammals for more than a decade, assisting with research, rescue and retrieval efforts of ill, injured or diseased manatees. Boats are equipped with propeller guards of the protection of the mammals. Humans and their boats are the biggest danger for full-grown manatees.

Manatee World President, Capt. David Tinder, said there are only about 2,600 manatees in the wild.

The gentle giants live to eat and to sleep, preferring water that is 68-70 degrees. In the summer, they might follow the warm water as far north as Florida's Panhandle or even to New England on the Atlantic Coast. They head south in fall. During the summer months, watch for them along the shore in Venice or Sarasota.

When feeding, they come up for air every few minutes. Because they eat from 10-30 percent of their body weight each day, you will have plenty of chances to see manatees on these boat trips. Their noses look like half coconuts from a distance.

Photo by Kim Cool

This cooling arbor is one of the vistas in the display gardens of the Naples Botanical Garden.

Take Interstate 75 to Exit 107 (Naples). Turn left onto Livingston Road, then right on to Radio Road (CR 856 West) for 1 mile. Turn left on to Airport Pulling Road (CR 31 South) and then right on to Francis Avenue. Turn left on to Shadowlawn Drive for .3 miles and then slight right on to Bayshore. Travel 1.5 miles to Thomasson to parking lot.

Naples Botanical Garden

If the best things come in small packages then the Naples Botanical Gardens is a diamond in the rough. In its second decade it has become an affiliate of the 75-year old Cleveland, Ohio Botanical garden, even sharing its executive director.

Still growing, the southern partner is located on the corner of Bayshore and Thomasson Drive in Naples. Look for new plants against a new stucco wall that surrounds the garden along both roads. The entrance to the parking lot is from Thomasson Drive. The garden recently added 148 contiguous acres to its site and is expected to become one of the finest collections of tropical and subtropical plants in the world.

Despite its size, the garden has a full program of classes and other programs and a variety of garden settings designed to inspire home gardeners and to educate children and adults about the environment of South Florida and especially is ecology.

Study fruit trees, palms, orchids, flowering trees, xerophytes, aroids, roses, begonias, bromeliads and native plants. There are examples galore both in the gardens and in the demonstration and classroom building.

There also is a Pine Flatwoods area nearby where you can walk nearly two miles of trails while learning how to save one of Southwest Florida's most treasured ecosystems.

Classes include everything from floral arranging to the garden's taste for travel programs, which generally focus on travel to similar tropical and sub tropical areas of the world.

Handheld computers are available to guests to use while walking through the gardens, facilitating the identification of the garden's tropical flora. In the two-acre Tropical Mosaic Garden, there are more than 600 plant species.

For more information, call (239) 643-7275 or visit www.naplesbotanicalgarden.org.

Photo by Kim Cool

For art's sake in Naples.

The Naples Museum of Art is generally open Tuesday-Saturday, 10 a.m.-4 p.m. and on Sunday in season. For more information, call (239) 597-1111 or visit www.thephil.org. Take Interstate 75 to Exit 107. Travel west on Pine Ridge to U.S. 41 and then go north to the next traffic light, at Pelican Bay Boulevard South. Turn left. The museum will be one block ahead, on the left.

Naples Philharmonic Center

The newest major museum in Florida has already become an old hand at bringing some of the finest art in the world to Southwest Florida. The three-story, 30,000-square foot museum opened on Nov. 7, 2000.

Recent shows have included major works by famed glass artist Dale Chihuly, impressionist and op art movement founder Victor Vasarely, Matisse, Picasso, Masterworks of French Painting and Sculpture from the Baltimore Museum of Art, the work of Winslow Homer, Joyce Tennyson, Edward Weston, Andy Warhol and others.

Guided by chairman, CEO and founder Myra Janco Daniels, the museum has become the place to see collections rarely seen all together in one place. The main thrust of this museum is to assemble collections of major works by artists of such renown that their works are scattered around the world, one here, two there and so on.

The Vasarely show, as an example, was the first United States retrospective of the artist to be held since the 1970s. It was organized by the museum in conjunction with the Vasarely estate. Theme shows such as Matisse, Picasso & Friends: Impressionism to Surrealism, Masterworks of French Painting and Sculpture from the Baltimore Museum of Art, which was featured in the 2004-2005 winter season are another type of show regularly planned to fill the museum's stunning interior.

Smaller shows augment the big shows, so that there always is something worth seeing within this museum's 15 galleries.

Permanent holdings include 277 paintings and drawings by American masters from 1900-1955, an extensive holding of modern Mexican art and one of the world's largest collections of miniatures. A glass-dome conservatory is highlighted by a 10-foot wide red chandelier designed by Chihuly.

The museum is a division of the Philharmonic Center for the Arts, Naples' performing arts center.

Photo by Kim Cool

The Sugden Community Theatre, 701 Fifth Ave., Naples,
is the home of the Naples Players, one of many theatrical companies in the Port Charlotte, Fort Myers and Naples area. Check
with the individual entertainment venues listed on the opposite
page for the latest offerings in the area.

Performing Arts Venues

Broadway Palm Dinner Theatre, 1380 Colonial Blvd., Fort Myers. (239) 278-4422

Charlotte Players, 701 Carmalita St., Punta Gorda (941) 505-7469

Cultural Park Theatre Co., 528 Cultural Park Blvd., Cape Coral (239) 772-5862

Florida Gulf Coast Univ. Arts Complex Black Box Theatre (239) 590-7150

Florida Repertory Theater, 2267 First St., Fort Myers www.floridarrep.org (239) 332-4488

Barbara B. Mann Performing Arts Hall, 8099 College Parkway (239) 481-4844

Naples Dinner Theatre, 1025 Piper Blvd., Naples .(239) 514-7827 or toll-free (877) 519-7827

Naples Philharmonic Ctr. for the Arts, 5833 Pelican Bay Blvd. www.thephil.org Tickets (239) 597-1900

Naples Players, Sugden Community Theatre, 701 Fifth Ave., Information (239) 261-5870 Tickets (239) 263-7990 www.gulfshoresplayhouse.org

Orpheus Players, 1165 Estero Blvd., Fort Myers Beach (239) 770-4299

Ths Schoolhouse Theater, 2200 Periwinkle Way, www.oldschoolhousetheater (239) 472-6862

Seminole Gulf Railway Dinner Train Theater, Colonial Station, off Colonial Boulevard & Metro Parkway, Fort Myers www.semgulf.com (239) 275-8487

Theatre Conspiracy, Foulds Theatre at the Lee County Alliance for the Arts, 10091 McGregor Blvd., Fort Myers www.theatreconspiracy.org

Photo by Kim Cool

It was hard enough to get tickets to see Boston Red Sox spring training games at the City of Palms Park in Fort Myers before the team won the World Series in 2004. With just two ballparks within 50 miles, it is a perennial problem in Fort Myers. If you do have tickets, you also have one of the best opportunities in baseball to secure player autographs and, there is plenty of shade in this park.

Professional Sports

American Hockey League AA hockey

Florida Everblades, Germain Arena,
11000 Everblades Parkway, Estero
http://www.floridaeverblades.com

Arena Football

Florida Firecats, Germain Arena
11000 Everblades Parkway, Estero
(239) 390-2287, www.floridafirecats.com.

Fencing

Fort Myers Fencing Club
4210 Fowler St., Unit 9, Fort Myers
www.fortunecity.com/olympia/giggs/263/HOMEx.html.

Baseball – Spring Training

Boston Red Sox, City of Palms Park
2201 Edison Ave, Fort Myers
(877)RED-SOXX
http://boston.redsox.mlb.com
Minnesota Twins, Bill Hammond Stadium
14100 Six Mile Cypress Parkway, Fort Myers,
Minnesota.twins.mlb.com

Minor League Baseball

Fort Myers Miracle, Bill Hammond Stadium
14100 Six Mile Cypress Parkway, Fort Myers
www.miraclebaseball.

Photo by Dennis Gardner

The Punta Gorda Depot was saved from the wrecking ball.
From Interstate 75, take Exit 179 (C.R. 769 Kings
Highway) toward Port Charlotte. Turn slight right and then left on
to U.S. 41 (Tamiami Trail) south. Turn slight left on to Carmalita
Street and then slight right from Carmalita Street on to Taylor
Road (CR 765). The depot is at 1009 Taylor. For more information,
visit www.charlotte-florida.com/community/historic.htm or call
(941) 639-6774.

Punta Gorda Train Depot

Count another victory for history. The Historic Venice Train Depot was saved. Now Punta Gorda is following suit.

Built in 1928, the slightly younger Punta Gorda Depot was the southernmost train station in the United States in that year. It is one of just six remaining depots built by the Atlantic Coast Line in the Mediterranean Revival style. The Venice depot also is Mediterranean Revival style.

The Punta Gorda Depot closed in 1971, slightly more than 20 years before the Venice Depot ceased welcoming trains. It was vacant for 25 years when the late Fred Babcock purchased the building and presented it to the local historical society.

Listed on the National Register of Historic Places, it was primarily a freight station with only a small area at the northern end of the building for passengers. Like the Venice Depot, it had racially separate waiting areas, restrooms and ticket windows — a sign of the time in which the two buildings were constructed. While complying with current building codes, the building was restored to its original state. The separate waiting rooms now house historical exhibits. In the Bernice A. Russell Colored Waiting Room Museum there are regular exhibits based on the history and culture of African-Americans in Charlotte County and Punta Gorda.

A handicap-accessible restroom and other historic exhibits now occupy what had been the "white" waiting room.

Plans call for railroad cars to be brought to the site at some point. The Venice Depot has a red caboose, serving the Venice Historical Society. There are plans for additional cars commemorating the circus history of that city.

The Punta Gorda Depot has an antique mall in the former freight room. Proceeds pay for maintenance and other projects of the society. For mall information, call (941) 639-6774.

Photo by Kim Cool

All aboard for murder and mayhem. Make your reservations in advance for the Seminole Gulf Railway. Trains depart from the Colonial Station in Fort Myers. From Interstate 75, travel 3 miles west on Colonial Boulevard to the mall at the Northwest corner of Colonial and the Metro Parkway. For prices, schedule and reservations, call (800) SEM-GULF or (239) 275-8487.

Seminole Gulf Railway

Wednesday-Sunday, the Seminole Gulf Railway train pulls out of the Fort Myers' Colonial Station with a killer aboard. It could that lady across the aisle from you for who but a heartless killer could wear such an outfit in public, but it also might be one of those strange folks that bursts into the car as you are taking your first sip of wine and nibbling on the appetizers at your table.

You may want to bone up on your Sherlock Holmes before stepping aboard the train. Be assured there will be some red herrings, none of which is one the menu.

Five dinner courses later, if you really pay attention, you should know who dunnit. If you do, there will be a prize. If not, you will just have to come back on another night and work on your detective skills.

The killers on this mystery train know no season, nor holiday, sometimes dressing for the occasion as a Christmas toy or Cupid. Arrows in the wrong hands can be deadly after all.

A typical dinner includes an appetizer of cheeses and grapes, corn chowder, garden salad, entree choices of chicken or prime rib or salmon, assorted breads and rolls, chocolate surprise for dessert plus coffee or tea. Mixed drinks, beer and wine can be ordered at an additional cost. Otherwise, the dinner and the mystery and the train ride are package-priced.

There are several overnight packages for those train fans who want to make more than a day or night of their ride. Most include lodging and visits to other area attractions.

Daylight trips, lasting about two hours, without mysteries are offered on Wednesdays and Saturdays during most of the year. These trips cross the Caloossahatchee River trestle and drawbridge to Bayshore, taking you past scenery that can only be seen from the train. Narrators add to the experience.

Photo courtesy of Billie Swamp Safari

Does Jonathan "Cattail" Vazquez or the alligator have the bigger smile at Billie Swamp Safari?

Take Interstate 75 to Exit 49 (Mobile Service Plaza) then go north 19 miles to the park entrance. For reservations or more information, call (800) 949-6101 or (863) 983-6101 or visit www.seminoletribe.com/safari.

Swamp Safari

In Big Cypress Swamp, on the Seminole Reservation, you can learn from the experts about one of the world's most intriguing environments, the water shed of the Everglades.

Billie Swamp Safari offers visitors a look at life on 2.200 lush acres of the reservation, tours into wetlands, hardwood hammocks and sloughs and a chance to see deer, water buffalo, bison, wild hogs, hawks, eagles and alligators in their native habitat. You might even see a rare Florida panther. Several live in the area.

Tours are offered on airboats or on swamp buggies. The buggies are customized vehicles that stand tall on high suspensions and big tires to give passengers an elevated view on their ride through the wetlands and cypress heads. The cypress dome boardwalk nature trail offers a third option.

Those who want to stay longer and learn even more can make reservations at Sam Jones Camp, named for the medicine man and leader of the Seminole resistors in the second Seminole War. Complete camping facilities are just a short ride from the safari area. Overnighters can stay in a native style chickee hut. Overnight packages include day and evening swamp tours, campfire stories and legends and more.

Spend at least a day for there is plenty to do here, from bird watching to visiting the herpetarium or witnessing alligator wrestling. Listening to stories about the unconquered Seminoles at a campfire chickee or simply rocking on the Swamp Water Cafe's porch are other ways to spend quality time on safari.

Be sure to try some gator nuggets at the cafe as well as Seminole specialties like frog legs, catfish and fry bread with honey. There also is an American-style menu.

Souvenirs are plentiful in the Billie Swamp Safari gift shop.

About the author

Kim Cool has written business, circus history, needlecraft, travel and ghost story books.

By day, the Sweet Briar College graduate writes about Venice, entertainment, homes and travel as the Features Editor of the *Venice Gondolier Sun*.

She is a member of the Venice Archives and Area Historical Collection, the Venice Historical Society, Historical Society of Sarasota County, The Circus Historical Society, the Advisory Board of

The author on a Florida Ever-Glides Sarasota guided Segway Tour.

the Salvation Army of Venice, a national synchronized, senior competition and gold test judge for United States Figure Skating, a former competitive curler at the national level and a charter member of the Florida Curling Club.

The writer has won awards from the Florida Press Association, Small Business Administration and Florida Press Club. She is listed in Who's Who of American Women, Who's Who in America, Who's Who in the World and other reference works.

Bibliography

Books

Baker, Rick. *Mangroves to Major League, a Timeline of St. Petersburg, Florida (Prehistory to 2000 A.D.* Southern Heritage Press. 2000.

Board, Prudy Taylor. *The Renaissance Vinoy, St. Petersburg's Crown Jewel.*The Donning Company Publishers.1999.

Byrd, Alan. *Florida Spring Training,* The Intrepid Traveler. 2004

Timepiece: Renaissance Vinoy Resort and Golf Club, published for the National Register of Historic Places.

Monaghan, Kelly. *The Other Orlando,* The Intrepid Traveler, 2002.

Watson, Jennifer and Dave and Allison Marx. *PassPorter Walt Disney World Resort,* PassPorter Travel Press, 2004.

Periodicals

St. Petersburg Times
Tampa Tribune
The Boca Beacon
The Bradenton Herald
The Fort Myers News Press
The Naples Daily News
The Port Charlotte Sun
The Venice Gondolier Sun
USAToday

Acknowledgments

This book would not have been written without the help of countless people who shared behind-the-scenes information about the parks and attractions included herein and the friends and colleagues who offered suggestions, came along for the ride and/or were willing to read the prepublication stories.

Others helped just by being there with me as I continue my magical adventure on the highways and byways of life.

I am especially grateful to Navteq for granting permission to use excerpts of the very excellent maps its cartographers create for the American Automobile Association. Good maps are road trip necessities.

It seems appropriate that my present journey as a collector of tales and adventures began at the Animal Kingdom Lodge bus stop at Walt Disney World on the anniversary of the 100th birthday of Walter Elias Disney, the man who created the modern theme park and brought the "World" to Florida.

When you come to a fork in the road, take it.

The people:

Charles J. Adams III, Rosemary Altea, Sam and Mike Altieri, David Brady, Chris and Rob Broyles, Pat and Trevor Charnley, Dan and Joan Conway, Marianna Czismadia, Dennis Gardner, Dave Herbst, Pat Garlausky Horwell, Pam Johnson, Chris and Susan Lockwood, Claude Lewis, Dan Mearns, Don Moore, Bob and Melinda Mudge, Peggi Paquette, Ella Patterson, Cliff Roles and Georgia Turner

Enjoy this excerpt from
Circus Days in Sarasota & Venice
another book of regional interest
from Historic Venice Press

It was 1968, time for Venice to begin clowning around seriously. Can a circus ever have enough clowns?

For The Greatest Show on Earth in the 1960s, having clowns at all was becoming a concern to owner Irvin Feld. Considering that a one-time clown named John Ringling was one of the great show's founders, it would not do to run out of clowns.

(The rare portrait of John Ringling as a clown is in the collection of circus memorabilia belonging to Robert Horne of Sarasota.)

As the circus approached its 10-year anniversary at its winter quarters in Venice, all was not right with The Greatest Show on Earth.

Times were changing.

Running away to join the circus was not something children of the 1960s did. Love beads, anti-war protests and hippies were the fashion in those early days of the Vietnam era. Children ran away to join a commune, not a circus.

The Greatest Show on Earth was down to just 14 clowns, a commodity referred to by the late P.T. Barnum as "the pegs on which to hang a circus."

The quickest way to succeed in any business is to identify a need and supply it.

Feld's solution to the diminishing supply of clowns was to open Clown College. If clowns were not swarming to the circus, the circus would train its own.

As the winter home of the Ringling show, Venice was gaining national and even international press. Clown College added yet another dimension to the city on the gulf.

Feld's college would safeguard the future of clowning in America and also dispel the notions of skeptics who felt that clowning was a God-given talent.

For three decades, despite the number of visiting snowbirds in search of Florida tans, each fall, white faces continued to be spotted around the town.

It was not unusual for a driver to pass a bicyclist, look in the rear view mirror and discover a clown face. I know, for I was one of those drivers.

Over on Miami Avenue, graduation photos appeared each November in the display windows of a local photography studio. The subjects were not clad in black drapes or dark suits but in colorful costumes, painted faces and outlandish hats and wigs. Those graduates marched to the beat of a different drummer.

The normal graduation procession was replaced by a performance of the class clowns. Consider that at Clown College every student was a class clown.

Invitations were coveted for the graduation performance, which offered a chance to see a future Emmett Kelly, Lou Jacobs or Frosty Little.

In fact, those attending the first graduation in 1968 did see Frosty Little. After several years of clowning, Little's acceptance to and graduation from Clown College paved the way for his stardom with The Greatest Show on Earth and to his eventual selection as a master clown, one of just four clowns ever awarded that honor.

Little was 42 when he entered that first class at Clown College, possibly one of the oldest students to ever attend the celebrated school. In most classes, the average age was closer to 20, but Little quickly made up for lost time, becoming Boss Clown on the Red Unit within two years of his graduation and Director of Clowns for the Red and Blue Units 10 years after that. He supervised 75 clowns in the two shows, helped develop new acts and annually spent a few months in Venice as a teacher at his alma mater, Clown College.

"They put us (he and his wife Pat) in a house on Center Road," Little said. "It always had a pool.

"I really enjoyed the show. It was so exciting."

The other three Master Clowns were the late Bobby Kay, Otto Greibling and Lou Jacobs, all Sarasota residents, and all destined to be showered with honors for their work.

Jacobs and Greibling have been honored at the Ringling Museum of the Circus, Circus Celebrity Nights; Jacobs in 1980 and Greibling in 2004. Greibling's award was given posthumously as a great performer of the Circus Past.

Greibling, born in 1896, began his career as an apprentice bareback rider with the Hodgini Riding Act, toured awhile with Tom Mix, and finally switching to clowning after suffering a bad fall. He joined the Ringling show in 1951, becoming known for several acts, including his "metal pie plate act."

In 1970, his larynx was removed because of cancer and he spent the last two years of his life miming for real instead of for fun as he had the previous 40 years of his career.

"I didn't know he didn't have a voice," said Clown College student Steve Smith. "He communicated that well. Everything he did was perfection. Bauman (Charly Bauman — the animal trainer and star of the Blue Unit in which Greibling performed) let us leave the curtains open so we could see Otto do his pie act. I have one of his tin plates on the wall of my office and sometimes I take it down and hold it next to me. Everything he did, he did to give everyone a big hug."

To even be considered for the honor, a clown had to be employed with the circus for a minimum of 15 years, something that became increasingly difficult each year that another class graduated from this most unique college.

One Clown College graduate has been employed by Ringling ever since his graduation in 1971 but he has little hope of ever being named a master clown.

Tim Holst got off to a rocky start. When I first spoke to him he asked if I wanted the "real story" or the one that was in the papers over the years.

Opting for the "real story," I learned that Holst was very nearly a Clown College dropout.

"They didn't like me,' he said. "But I came from a Mormon family in Utah and could not go home and tell my parents that I had failed out of Clown College. instead I begged and promised that if I could finish the course, I would leave and never bother them (Clown College) again. As soon as graduation was over, I headed for home."

Back in Utah, Holst got a phone call.

"Where are you?" the caller said. "We were going to give you a contract."

He went right back to Venice. Holst worked as a clown for two years before auditioning for and winning the job of ringmaster of the Red Unit, one of the most important jobs in the circus.

The ringmaster keeps the show going, singing the major songs to introduce the big production numbers, announcing the acts and, most important of all, keeping things calm if there ever is any kind of emergency.

Eventually the man they "didn't like" worked his way up the ladder to become a Ringling vice president.

Logging more than a million miles in the air each year, Holst travels the world in search of new acts for the circus.

Only recently did he learn that he had two uncles who also were associated with the circus — as bill posters (advance men who traveled ahead of the show to post bills (advertising signs) to announce the impending arrival of a show).

Like Smith, the trainmaster; Gebel-Williams, the famous animal trainer, fellow clowns Otto Greibling and Lou Jacobs,

Holst was honored as a Circus Celebrity by the Ringling Museum of the Circus. His award, in 2004, was for being a Power Behind the Scenes.

"I learned circus by transfusion," Holst said. "I learned a lot from Charly Bauman. He had an eye for what was right. The devotion he had for his animals was something to see. I learned passion and hard work from Charlie Smith, who made sure I always had water."

(In the early days, every circus employee had a bucket of water a day for washing. Each performer's name was on his bucket.)

Holst's award was presented to him by Steve Smith, another member of the Class of 1971 at Clown College.

"That two more unlikely schlubs would lead such a life," Smith said. "Only in America could a little short guy from Zanesville, Ohio, wind up as director of Clown College. And only in American could a Mormon from Galesburg, Ill., wander into Venice and do so well."

Newer Venice resident, Dennis Hall, was in the class of 1972 at Clown College, landing a contract to tour with the Ringling show's Blue Unit in 1973.

"In the Blue Unit, we had Charly Bauman," he said. "He was classy but different than Gunther. In the Blue Unit, everybody had a piece of the spotlight.

"I thought I'd made a career," he said."Alvin Bale was going to teach me the rocket."

Instead, he left the show after one year and headed back to Boston, where he ended up teaching clowning in an adult education program for seven years.

"I've done a ton of things," he said at the age of 55. "To this day I am trying to get back on the show. I'd still like to become a human projectile."

Hall has worked as a carpenter and as a house painter, skills he put to use even as a tramp clown, decorating his own Ringling train compartment to his taste.

As Clown College became more well-known, applications soared to more than 5,000 in a single year. From that number no more than 60 would be selected for the tuition-free program. Students paid their own living expenses and immersed themselves totally in clowning 24 hours a day, seven days a week. They had to be at least 17 years and they had to be U.S. citizens. Auditions were held in major cities throughout the country but some were accepted based on extensive written applications. Potential student clowns were "carefully evaluated for raw talent, motivation, flexibility and aptitude for hard work and improvisation."

Creativity was a must.

No sooner had Clown College graduated its first class than an edict was handed down from Feld.

" ...In 1969, all the clowns were informed that at the end of each two-year run, and the show would be revamped for another season, all the clown gags would be 'stored away' and all new gags would be used," Frosty Little said. "In those days we had between 25-35 clowns on each unit and used about 50 gags. I would get new gags from our 'gag' sessions, but never enough for the shows. We would get some more from the Clown College classes, but we still wouldn't have enough, so the producing clown would have to think up even more.

"Every time the clowns got a little spare time, in between the many hours of production rehearsals, we would be painting, building, sewing, etc.," Little continued "In addition carpenter George Shellenberger, painter Ivan Saxby and six additional sewing ladies were all assisting us to get the gags ready. At 6 p.m. on Clown Night, all the clowns came out in their

157

'Agent's Suits' (best costume). The circus owner, his assistant, the performance director and a few others people were seated behind a table. They would give the signal to begin. I would bring out one clown at a time. The clown would stand in front of the table to be critiqued on his costume and makeup. The critique was very tough, as it should be, since this was The Greatest Show on Earth."

After the critique session, Little would meet with the director of Clown College. While the clowns all went out to a chicken dinner at a Venice restaurant, Little and the director would meet with the president of the circus to discuss which gags would be kept for the show.

Usually, about half would be accepted and the clowns would have to get back to work to find 25 more new gags. Just six days remained at that time before rehearsals would begin.

"During the six days we hade to develop new gags, build and paint the props, get the proper wardrobe and rehearse the gags," Little said. "This week was called Hell Week."

In the 1970s and 1980s, rehearsals began at 7 p.m. and ran until about 10 p.m., followed by meetings of department heads with the president of the circus, until nearly 1 a.m. Gags would be thrown out, and first thing in the morning the sewing ladies would be hard at work on new costumes for the new gags.

"Many times we would be painting right up to the time of the second dress rehearsal," Little said.

Because of the humidity in the Venice winter quarters from its proximity to the gulf, painters used a lot of Japan dryer agent in their paints to speed up drying time on new props.

Had they known what came with the coveted contract, would so many have applied to Clown College?

In 1983, a typical year, 45 students were selected from a pool of 5,289 applicants; seven were females. They ranged in age from 17 to 28, in weight from 80 to 200 pounds and in height from 3 feet 8 inches tall to 6 feet 6 inches tall. They came from 20 states. It was considered more difficult to get into Clown College than medical school.

During the nine-week session, students learned make-up, designing their own clown face in the process; studied juggling, stiltwalking and gymnastics; and developed new gags they would use at graduation and later.

In several interviews given over his lengthy career, Little was quoted as saying that gags are "the essence of the art," further defining gags as "cartoons come to life." According to him, the best gags were based on real life but taken one step farther.

In an article that appeared in the Venice Gondolier Sun's Oct. 5, 1983 edition, Little described a gag about a mother being annoyed by her little boy. She buys him a balloon and he proceeds to break it. Then he hits her and she spanks him. That is the real-life situation that most people can relate to. This scenario became a gag when, in the circus ring, the little boy was hooked to a balloon, raised in the air and disappeared.

Faculty

Little and a cadre of other professional clowns, make-up and costume experts plus acting coaches, comprised the 30 or so faculty members of the college. Like any college there was a dean. There also were several visiting professors and guest lecturers.

Jacobs, considered a living legend in those days, was one of the visiting professors, spending at least one day each term with the students, even when he was well into his 80s. It seemed fitting that Jacobs would end his career in Florida since he made his debut, at the age of 7, playing the hindquarters of an alligator. His brother was the front.

Jacobs came to the United States in 1923, joining the Ringling show two years later. He is the creator of the circus' famous midget car act — one of the most popular gags in the history of clowning. He joined the Clown College faculty in 1974. Jacobs died in 1992. He was 89. (His daughter Dolly is one of the founders of Circus Sarasota)

Another of the great clowns who taught at Clown College was Otto Greibling, a tramp clown who had extensive experience in some of the top circuses in the world, eventually joining the Ringling show in 1951.

Greibling stayed with Ringling right up until his death in 1972, teaching at Clown College during its early years.

Other faculty members included Florida Studio Theatre managing artistic director Richard Hopkins, who taught the art of improvisation, a skill possibly more important for clowns than for actors.

Consider that whenever an emergency of any kind occurs in the circus, it is the clowns that must improvise in order to calm the crowds, help them to escape if need be, or simply distract them for a time while some mishap is righted.

Another prominent Sarasota name involved in Clown College beginning in 1984 was the late Vicki Holden, who went on to become the chief costume designer of the Asolo Theatre Company in Sarasota. In her first year on the faculty of Clown College, she taught wig construction to the student clowns.

All this history and more was crammed into the college's two-month program. More is contained in the book, *Circus Days in Sarasota & Venice*. Order it now.

HISTORIC VENICE PRESS
ORDER FORM

Ghost Stories of Sarasota..$12.95
     ISBN 0-9721655-1-7

Ghost Stories of Venice..$9.95
     ISBN 0-9721655-0-9

Circus Days in Sarasota & Venice...$18.95
     ISBN 0-9721655-3-3

Ghost Stories of Clearwater & St Petersburg............................$12.95
     ISBN 0-9721655-4-1

Cool Road Trips in SW Florida...$12.95
     ISBN 0-9721655-6-8

Indicate the number of books you wish to order below:

Number   Total
ordered

_____ Sarasota @ 12.95   _____
_____ Venice @ 8.95   _____
_____ Circus Days@ 18.95   _____
_____ Clearwater & St. Petersburg @ 12.95
_____ Cool RoadTrips in SW Florida @ 12.95

Sub total _____

Florida residents add 7 percent sales tax _____

Shipping to one address   _____ N/C

Total amount enclosed: _____

Mail to:

HISTORIC VENICE PRESS
PO Box 800
Venice, FL 34284

Afterword

Florida is filled with endless road trip possibilities and several railroad trip possibilities. This first collection of interesting destinations in and around SW Florida is just the beginning. Next on the list will be *Cool Road Trips in Central Florida* and *Cool Road Trips in SE Florida*. If you have suggestions for places to see and visit anywhere in this wonderful state, please contact me by e-mail at: Kimcool@www.historicvenicepress.com or by regular mail to Kim Cool at:

Historic Venice Press
PO Box 800
Venice, FL 34284

I hope you enjoy trippin' through SW Florida.

Kim Cool
Venice, Florida
June 2005